D0434775

THE 1988 DEFENSE BUDGET

Studies in Defense Policy

SELECTED TITLES

THE 1988 DEFENSE BUDGET

Joshua M. Epstein

THE BROOKINGS INSTITUTION
Washington, D.C.

Copyright © 1987 by
THE BROOKINGS INSTITUTION
1775 Massachusetts Avenue, NW. Washington, D.C. 20036

Library of Congress Catalog Card Number 87-71176

ISBN 0-8157-2459-4

9 8 7 6 5 4 3 2 1

LIBRARY
The University of Texas
At San Antonio

Board of Trustees
Louis W. Cabot
Chairman
Ralph S. Saul
Vice Chairman;
Chairman, Executive Committee;
Chairman, Development Committee
Samuel H. Armacost
J. David Barnes
Rex J. Bates
A. W. Clausen
William T. Coleman, Jr.
Richard G. Darman
Thomas R. Donahue
Charles W. Duncan, Jr.
Walter Y. Elisha
Robert F. Erburu
Roberto C. Goizueta
Robert D. Haas
Philip M. Hawley
Roy M. Huffington
B. R. Inman
Vernon E. Jordan, Jr.
James A. Joseph
James T. Lynn
Donald F. McHenry
Bruce K. MacLaury
Mary Patterson McPherson
Maconda B. O'Connor
Donald S. Perkins
J. Woodward Redmond
James D. Robinson III
Robert V. Roosa
B. Francis Saul II
Henry B. Schacht
Howard R. Swearer
Morris Tanenbaum
James D. Wolfensohn
Ezra K. Zilkha
Charles J. Zwick

Honorary Trustees
Vincent M. Barnett, Jr.
Barton M. Biggs
Eugene R. Black
Robert D. Calkins
Edward W. Carter
Frank T. Cary
Lloyd N. Cutler
Bruce B. Dayton
Douglas Dillon
Huntington Harris
Andrew Heiskell
Roger W. Heyns
John E. Lockwood
William McC. Martin, Jr.
Robert S. McNamara
Arjay Miller
Charles W. Robinson
H. Chapman Rose
Gerard C. Smith
Robert Brookings Smith
Sydney Stein, Jr.
Phyllis A. Wallace

THE BROOKINGS INSTITUTION is an independent organization devoted to nonpartisan research, education, and publication in economics, government, foreign policy, and the social sciences generally. Its principal purposes are to aid in the development of sound public policies and to promote public understanding of issues of national importance.

The Institution was founded on December 8, 1927, to merge the activities of the Institute for Government Research, founded in 1916, the Institute of Economics, founded in 1922, and the Robert Brookings Graduate School of Economics and Government, founded in 1924.

The Board of Trustees is responsible for the general administration of the Institution, while the immediate direction of the policies, program, and staff is vested in the President, assisted by an advisory committee of the officers and staff. The by-laws of the Institution state: "It is the function of the Trustees to make possible the conduct of scientific research, and publication, under the most favorable conditions, and to safeguard the independence of the research staff in the pursuit of their studies and in the publication of the results of such studies. It is not a part of their function to determine, control, or influence the conduct of particular investigations or the conclusions reached."

The President bears final responsibility for the decision to publish a manuscript as a Brookings book. In reaching his judgment on the competence, accuracy, and objectivity of each study, the President is advised by the director of the appropriate research program and weighs the views of a panel of expert outside readers who report to him in confidence on the quality of the work. Publication of a work signifies that it is deemed a competent treatment worthy of public consideration but does not imply endorsement of conclusions or recommendations.

The Institution maintains its position of neutrality on issues of public policy in order to safeguard the intellectual freedom of the staff. Hence interpretations or conclusions in Brookings publications should be understood to be solely those of the authors and should not be attributed to the Institution, to its trustees, officers, or other staff members, or to the organizations that support its research.

FOREWORD

THE same factors that led Congress to reduce the defense budget for fiscal years 1986 and 1987 are present again this year: intense pressure to lower the federal deficit, congressional unwillingness to cut spending on domestic social programs, and the president's refusal to raise taxes. As a result, there is general agreement that the Reagan administration's defense goals will not all be achieved. No consensus exists, however, on which of the competing programs—from a space-based defense of the United States to the conventional ground defense of Western Europe—deserve priority.

Meanwhile, during the past year, one arms control treaty has been abandoned (SALT II), another is under severe strain (the ABM Treaty), while yet others are newly proposed (for intermediate nuclear forces in Europe). Rarely, it would seem, has force planning been in such a state of flux. Under the circumstances, clear thinking about the military balance, security priorities, and the relative efficiency of competing alternatives is especially needed.

In this study, Joshua M. Epstein, a research associate in the Brookings Foreign Policy Studies program, challenges the administration's priorities, identifies inefficiencies in its defense proposals, and presents an alternative defense plan. After systematically assessing U.S. nuclear and conventional requirements, he offers specific recommendations that would save nearly $50 billion over two years without detriment to the security of the United States or its allies.

The author acknowledges the valuable suggestions of John D. Steinbruner, Paul B. Stares, Martin Binkin, Charles L. Schultze, and Barry M. Blechman. He also extends deep thanks to Lisa B. Mages for research assistance, to Daniel A. Lindley III for verifying references and tables, to Ann M. Ziegler for secretarial support, to Caroline Lalire for editing the manuscript, and to Carole H. Newman and Sallyjune F. Kuka of the Brookings Social Science Computation Center for computer graphics.

This study was funded by grants from the Ford Foundation and the John D. and Catherine T. MacArthur Foundation. Brookings is grateful for this support.

The views expressed are those of the author and should not be ascribed to the persons or foundations whose assistance is acknowledged or to the trustees, officers, or other staff members of the Brookings Institution.

BRUCE K. MACLAURY
President

May 1987
Washington, D.C.

THE 1988 DEFENSE BUDGET

THE LARGEST peacetime military buildup in American history is apparently over. Following unprecedented growth in defense appropriations from 1981 through 1985, to levels surpassing those of the peak Vietnam years, Congress imposed a real reduction of 4.2 percent in fiscal 1986, and another reduction of 2.5 percent in fiscal 1987. Compared with the Reagan administration's defense boom years of 1981 and 1982—in which growth rates of 12 percent were recorded—these cuts represented a major reversal (figures 1 and 2).

Many factors contributed to the turnaround. For one, the Central Intelligence Agency reassessed the growth rate in Soviet military spending in 1983. In contrast to the relentless buildup that had been portrayed—and that had undergirded the Pentagon's budget requests—the Soviets were found to have cut their real defense growth rate in half, from 4 to 5 percent (for 1970–76) to 2 percent a year from 1976 to 1983. Especially notable was the CIA's finding that Soviet military procurement in particular was stagnant; it did not grow at all in real terms for the entire seven-year period.

Not only were the Soviets spending less than had been claimed, but numerous Pentagon procurement "horror stories" called into question the efficiency with which the Defense Department was managing its own funds. To the infamous overpriced coffee pots and toilet seats were added the more significant testing distortions and operational failures of the Sergeant York divisional air defense (DIVAD) system, which, under duress, the Pentagon cancelled, and the Bradley fighting vehicle.[1]

---

1. A November 1986 General Accounting Office report characterized the Bradley as being more vulnerable to antiarmor weapons than its predecessor, the M113 armored personnel carrier. It has also been charged that the Bradley would be unable to ford rivers and streams during combat. See General Accounting Office. *Bradley Vehicle:*

1

Figure 1. Defense Budget Authority and Outlays, Fiscal Years 1950–92ᵃ
Billions of 1988 dollars

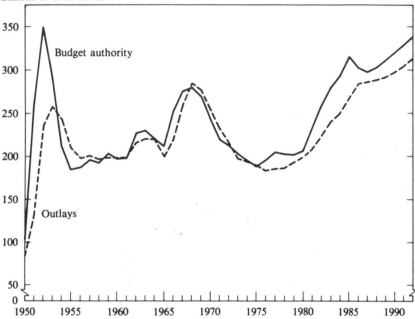

Source: Unpublished material provided by the Office of Management and Budget. The numbers for 1987–92 reflect the president's fiscal 1988 budget request.
a. Comprises the Department of Defense military subfunction (051).

Today's serious problems with the B-1 bomber,[2] a cornerstone of the Reagan buildup, have merely enforced the impression of managerial laxity.

The single most powerful downward pressure on the defense budget, however, has been the federal deficit, which climbed to unprecedented

---

Army's Efforts to Make It More Survivable (Washington, D.C.: GAO, 1986); Fred Kaplan, "GAO Calls the Army's New Troop Carrier Vulnerable," *Boston Globe,* November 6, 1986; John H. Cushman, Jr., "Experts See Risk in Troop Carrier," *New York Times,* September 21, 1986; and John H. Cushman, Jr., "Suit Charges Contractor Lied to Army on Infantry Vehicle," *New York Times,* September 16, 1986.

2. The U.S. Air Force has requested $600 million in additional funds over the next three years for further modifications and testing of the B-1B bomber. Among the problems that have been encountered in the B-1B are a defensive avionics system that does not meet the required capability, major flight control problems during initial test flights, problems with the bomber's terrain-following radar, and leaks in the fuel tanks. See Molly Moore, "B1 Bomber Repair Fund Is Requested," *Washington Post,* January 7, 1987; and Molly Moore, "Defects Found in B1 Bomber," *Washington Post,* December 4, 1986.

Figure 2. Percent Annual Changes in Defense Funding, Fiscal Years 1977-89ᵃ

Percent change

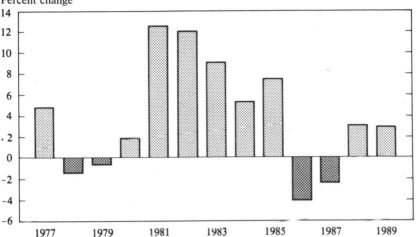

Source: Alice C. Maroni, *The Fiscal Year 1988 Defense Budget Request Data Summary*, Congressional Research Service Report 87-16F (CRS, 1987), p. 15. The 1987 figure is based on an estimate that excludes the supplemental budget request. The 1988 and 1989 figures represent the administration's two-year budget request.

a. Figures are for the National Defense Function (050), which comprises three subfunctions: Department of Defense military programs (051); Department of Energy atomic energy defense activities (053); and defense-related activities—civil defense, operation of the selective service system, and management and acquisition of the strategic stockpile (054).

levels—in absolute terms and as a percent of gross national product—during the Reagan defense buildup (table 1).

Given Congress's unwillingness, particularly in election years, to cut social security or medicare, and the president's refusal to sanction a tax increase, it was inevitable that defense would bear an important burden in deficit reduction. Though it no longer has the force of law, a strict interpretation of the 1985 Balanced Budget and Emergency Deficit Control Act, also known as Gramm-Rudman-Hollings, would require defense reductions in fiscal 1988 of 14 percent from the 1987 level.[3] Such drastic reductions are implausible. But given Democratic control of both houses of Congress, the Reagan administration is unlikely to be granted any increase beyond inflation in 1988; some doubt it will get that. Barring a revolutionary change in the international environment, a budget constraint of zero real growth (at most) appears to be in place.

In practical terms, this means that not all the administration's original goals are achievable: rapid across-the-board modernization of all legs of

3. These reductions would be in outlays. Congressional Budget Office, *The Economic and Budget Outlook: Fiscal Years 1988-1992*, 1987 Annual Report, pt. 1 (CBO, 1987), p. xx.

**Table 1. Federal Government Surpluses or Deficits in Absolute Amounts
and as Percentages of Gross National Product, Fiscal Years 1950–92**
Billions of dollars unless otherwise specified

Year	Total federal surplus or deficit	Surplus or deficit as percent of GNP	Year	Total federal surplus or deficit	Surplus or deficit as percent of GNP
1950	− 3.1	− 1.2	1972	− 23.4	− 2.0
1951	6.1	1.9	1973	− 14.9	− 1.2
1952	− 1.5	− 0.4	1974	− 6.1	− 0.4
1953	− 6.5	− 1.8	1975	− 53.2	− 3.5
1954	− 1.2	− 0.3	1976	− 73.7	− 4.3
1955	− 3.0	− 0.8	TQ[a]	− 14.7	− 3.3
1956	3.9	0.9	1977	− 53.6	− 2.8
1957	3.4	0.8	1978	− 59.2	− 2.7
1958	− 2.8	− 0.6	1979	− 40.2	− 1.6
1959	− 12.8	− 2.7	1980	− 73.8	− 2.8
1960	0.3	0.1	1981	− 78.9	− 2.6
1961	− 3.3	− 0.6	1982	− 127.9	− 4.1
1962	− 7.1	− 1.3	1983	− 207.8	− 6.3
1963	− 4.8	− 0.8	1984	− 185.3	− 5.0
1964	− 5.9	− 0.9	1985	− 212.3	− 5.4
1965	− 1.4	− 0.2	1986	− 220.7	− 5.3
1966	− 3.7	− 0.5	1987	− 174.0	− 4.0
1967	− 8.6	− 1.1	1988	− 169.0	− 3.6
1968	− 25.2	− 3.0	1989	− 162.0	− 3.2
1969	3.2	0.3	1990	− 134.0	− 2.5
1970	− 2.8	− 0.3	1991	− 109.0	− 1.9
1971	− 23.0	− 2.2	1992	− 85.0	− 1.4

Sources: 1950–86 figures are from Office of Management and Budget, *Historical Tables, Budget of the United States Government, Fiscal Year 1988* (Government Printing Office, 1987), pp. 15.6(1), 15.6(2); 1987–92 projections are from Congressional Budget Office, *The Economic and Budget Outlook: Fiscal Years 1988–1992,* 1987 Annual Report, pt. 1 (CBO, 1987), pp. xiv, 7.
a. Fiscal 1976 transition quarter (July through September).

the strategic offensive triad (intercontinental ballistic missiles, bombers, and submarines); vigorous development of antisatellite capabilities and space-based strategic defenses; modernization of the ground and tactical air forces, with an expansion of the latter to 40 wings; and a 600-ship navy built around 15 large-deck aircraft carrier battlegroups—everything buttressed by a vibrant research and development base, with growing readiness and sustainability for all. Some things will have to give.

Despite a modest accommodation to these fiscal pressures—evident in the administration's 1988 request (tables 3 and 4 below) for a 3 percent real increase in the defense budget—the Pentagon has not come to grips with the problem of choice, or adjusted its priorities in any fundamental way. Continued rapid growth in funding for strategic offensive force modernization (featuring two new intercontinental ballistic missiles [ICBMs], two bombers, and new Trident submarines and missiles), the strategic defense initiative, and two new aircraft carriers would be paid for largely through reductions or decreases in the pace (stretchouts) of other conventional programs (table 2). But are those the right priorities? And if not, how should the defense budget request be altered? More important, can adequate security be provided without growth in defense spending?

A rational attack on that problem requires several logical steps. The first is to identify the core missions for which U.S. forces are designed. In macroeconomic, or large-scale budgeting, terms, these missions are the conventional defense of Western Europe, the Persian Gulf, South Korea, and the air-lanes and sea-lanes to those theaters of war.[4] Overarching these major conventional contingencies is the requirement to deter nuclear attack on the United States and its allies and to terminate nuclear exchanges with minimal damage if deterrence fails. Second, using methods that go beyond the static comparison of peacetime inventories, one attempts to assess the forces' performance in executing these basic missions. Finally, on the basis of these dynamic campaign analyses, one cuts what is superfluous and attempts to rectify any outstanding deficiencies in the most efficient manner.

When this contingency-based assessment is conducted rigorously, some troublesome features of the Reagan administration's defense buildup become evident: exaggerated assessments of Soviet strength; the adoption of strategies (especially naval) that may be infeasible and escalatory; excessive pace in programs of doubtful urgency; inefficient duplications of effort; and questionable priorities.

It is this study's main thesis that the United States can satisfy its

4. Though Europe, the Persian Gulf, and Korea are the specific focal points of U.S. conventional force planning, larger alliance or regional security issues, or both, are presumed to be at stake. For example, the security of Israel and Saudi Arabia is of concern in the Persian Gulf and general Southwest Asian context, though for force planning and budgeting purposes a Soviet invasion of Iran is the dominant regional contingency. Similarly, the security of Japan is presumed to be enhanced by a strong U.S. military presence in northeast Asia, though the direct defense of South Korea is (like Iran) the most demanding and prominent of the force planning contingencies.

Table 2.   Selected Strategic and Conventional Programs, Fiscal Years 1987–88[a]

Program	Strategic program costs (millions of dollars)		
	1987 estimate	1988 request	Percent change
MX Missile	1,541.2	1,905.1	23.6
Small ICBM (Midgetman)	1,168.7	2,257.0	93.1
Trident II missile	2,961.8	3,528.5	19.1
B-1B bomber	112.8	415.5	268.4
Stealth bomber (estimate)	4,150.0	4,760.0	14.7
Strategic defense initiative	3,743.4	5,230.8	39.7
Space defense system (antisatellite)	189.3	440.2	132.5
Atomic energy defense activities (Department of Energy)	7,478.0	8,050.0	7.6

Program	Conventional program quantities		
	1987 projection for 1988	1988 request for 1988	Percent change
AH-64 Apache helicopter ·	78	67	– 14.1
UH-60 Blackhawk helicopter	85	61	– 28.2
F/A 18 Hornet	132	84	– 36.4
M1 Abrams Tank	840	600	– 28.6
M2 Bradley fighting vehicle	870	616	– 29.2
High-mobility multipurpose wheeled vehicle (HMMWV)	4,555	3,674	– 19.3
High-speed antiradiation missile (HARM)	3,024	2,514	– 16.9
AV-8B Harrier	42	32	– 23.8
EA-6B Prowler	12	6	– 50.0
MK-48 advancd capabilities (ADCAP) torpedo	296	100	– 66.2
F-15 Eagle	48	42	– 12.5
F-16 Falcon	216	180	– 16.7
Advanced medium-range air-to-air missile (AMRAAM)	833	630	– 24.4
IIR Maverick missile	7,927	2,701	– 65.9

Sources: For strategic programs, *Department of Defense Annual Report to the Congress, Fiscal Year 1988* (GPO, 1987), pp. 206, 209, 212; Department of Defense, *Program Acquisition Costs by Weapon System, Department of Defense Budget for Fiscal Years 1988 and 1989* (DOD, 1987), pp. ii, iv, v, viii, ix; OMB, *Historical Tables, Fiscal Year 1988*, p. 5.1(2); and Joseph F. Campbell, "Stealth Bomber: Program on Track, Growth for Northrop," Paine Webber Status Report, February 13, 1986, p. 3. For conventional programs, Center on Budget and Policy Priorities, Defense Budget Project, "The FY 1988 Defense Budget: Preliminary Analysis" (January 6, 1987), table 6. For a more complete description of the administration's fiscal 1988 and 1989 defense budget, see DOD's *Annual Report* and *Program Acquisition Costs* mentioned above; DOD, *Procurement Programs (P-1), Department of Defense Budget for Fiscal Years 1988 and 1989;* and DOD, *R, D, T, & E Programs (R-1), Department of Defense Budget for Fiscal Years 1988 and 1989.*

a. Growth in strategic programs from 1987 to 1988 is measured in budget authority rather than in weapon systems because many major strategic systems are in development and not yet in the procurement phase. Stretchouts or reductions of conventional programs, by contrast, can be measured by changes in the quantities of weapons requested from one year to the next.

security commitments with no real increase in defense spending if these shortcomings are rectified. Indeed, real reductions are possible without detriment to U.S. security.

The argument to that effect is presented below. While it is contingency based, it takes the Reagan budget request as a baseline, adding or subtracting elements. Theoretically, because every dollar spent on defense can ultimately be connected to some actual or potential military contingency, it is possible to construct the entire defense budget from contingency building blocks (defense of Europe, defense of the Persian Gulf, and so forth). Each budget module would include allowances for planned modernization, routine equipment replacements, and other investment costs, as well as all operating and support expenses. A "zero-based" defense budget so constructed would ideally equal the budget arrived at by subtracting programs from the proposed budget that are superfluous or inefficient or by shifting financial resources from over-funded to underfunded areas, or both. Although part of a longer-term effort to craft defense budgets by construction, this analysis is largely of the request-based, rather than zero-based, type. Key issues and contingencies are focused on, and budgetary alterations are recommended.

Before the key strategic nuclear and conventional policy issues facing Congress are presented, the administration's fiscal 1988 defense request and multiyear plan are examined, in the aggregate and broken down in different ways. Then certain structural features of defense spending are explained. Specifically, in any process, attempts to change course must contend with the momentum of decisions that have already been made. Despite congressional cutbacks, the momentum "stored" in the defense budget is still very great. This backlog of built-in spending is especially pronounced in defense. Since it represents an important constraint in deficit reduction and defense planning, this systemic feature of defense spending should be understood as context to any policy discussion.

The Budget Request and Momentum

The administration's five-year budget authority request and the actual defense expenditures, or outlays, that would result are shown in table 3. These totals can be disaggregated in any number of ways, such as by military service, by appropriation title, by program, and between nuclear and nonnuclear elements. One of the more revealing break-

Table 3. The Administration's Defense Budget Plan, Fiscal Years 1987–92[a]
Millions of dollars unless otherwise specified

Year	050 account	Real growth (percent)	051 account	Real growth (percent)
		Budget authority		
1987	289,700	. . .	281,695	. . .
1988	311,967	3.0	303,295	3.0
1989	332,364	2.9	323,290	3.0
1990	353,463	2.9	343,900	2.9
1991	374,979	2.9	364,900	2.9
1992	396,907	2.8	386,500	2.9
Five-year average	. . .	2.9	. . .	3.0
		Outlays		
1987	282,246	. . .	274,200	. . .
1988	297,550	0.7	289,300	0.8
1989	312,197	1.2	303,700	1.2
1990	329,983	2.0	321,000	2.0
1991	349,500	2.5	340,000	2.5
1992	370,851	3.0	361,000	3.1
Five-year average	. . .	1.9	. . .	1.9

Sources: OMB, *Historical Tables, Fiscal Year 1988*, pp. 3.3(4), 3.3(5), 5.1(2), 5.1(3); *Department of Defense Annual Report, Fiscal Year 1988*, p. 325; and information from OMB. The DOD deflators are calculated from Office of the Assistant Secretary of Defense (Comptroller), *National Defense Budget Estimates for FY 1988/1989* (OASD, 1987), pp. 54, 56.

a. The 050 account is for the National Defense Function; the 051 account is for the Department of Defense military programs. See figure 2, note a, for further explanation.

downs is between investment and operation and support (O&S) expenses (table 4).

The investment accounts are procurement; research, development, test, and evaluation; and military construction. In these appropriation titles are funds for the so-called big-ticket items—capital projects such as aircraft carriers, stealth bombers, MX missiles, and Star Wars technologies. Investment spending is intended largely to modernize or expand one's force, anticipating tomorrow's threat. For instance, stealth bomber supporters see the radar-evading plane as necessary to penetrate the Soviet air defenses projected for the 1990s and to attack mobile ballistic missiles deployed in the interim.

The Reagan buildup has been investment intensive; the ratio of investment spending to expenditures on operation and support of existing forces is more than 50 percent higher than the ratio recorded over the

Table 4. Defense Department Investment and Operation and Support Request,
Fiscal Years 1987–92
Millions of dollars

Category	Budget authority (051)					
	1987	1988	1989	1990	1991	1992
Investment						
Procurement	85,174	83,974	94,624	105,587	115,552	123,305
Research and development	35,994	43,719	44,203	39,586	39,652	42,278
Military construction	5,131	6,592	6,885	7,463	7,721	8,478
Subtotal	126,299	134,285	145,712	152,636	162,925	174,061
Operation and support						
Military personnel	73,761	76,299	76,632	78,336	78,923	79,265
Operation and maintenance	78,536	86,065	90,045	96,549	101,708	106,677
Family housing	3,121	3,484	3,679	4,005	4,047	4,324
Subtotal	155,418	165,848	170,356	178,890	184,678	190,266
Defense Department total[a]	281,695	303,295	323,290	343,900	364,900	386,500

Sources: OMB, *Historical Tables, Fiscal Year 1988*, pp. 5.1(2), 5.1(3); and *Department of Defense Annual Report, Fiscal Year 1988*, p. 325.

a. The total DOD request includes funds for "other" (revolving funds, offsetting receipts, and allowances for civilian and military pay raises and benefits and other legislation). "Other" funds are not included in either investment or operation and support categories for the purposes of this table.

1970s.[5] This change has noteworthy consequences because a long stream of spending commitments results from appropriations for investment, whereas a dollar appropriated for O&S is spent much more rapidly. The rates at which appropriations for investment and O&S are actually spent (their outlay rates) are shown in table 5. Because appropriations made in one year may require many years to spend, there is always a backlog of expenditures to which the Pentagon is committed from budget authority granted in prior years. In fact, even if defense appropriations (new budget authority) were zero for the next five years, national defense spending would total $200 billion, with investment accounting for almost all backlog spending after the first year (table 6).

5. Investment/O&S (1971–80) is 0.530; investment/O&S (Reagan, 1981–92) is 0.833; percent change is [(0.833 − 0.53)(100)]/(0.53) = 57. Ratios are derived from fiscal 1971–75 budget authority data from Office of the Assistant Secretary of Defense (Comptroller), *National Defense Budget Estimates for FY 1986* (DOD, 1985), pp. 85–86; and fiscal 1976–92 data from *Historical Tables, Budget of the United States Government, Fiscal Year 1988*, pp. 5.1(1)–5.1(3).

Table 5. Defense Outlay Rates by Appropriation Title, Fiscal Year 1988
Percent of first-year budget authority spent

	Year					
Appropriation title	First	Second	Third	Fourth	Fifth	Sixth
"Slow-money" investment accounts						
Procurement	15.00	30.17	26.69	13.59	6.30	1.24
Research, development, test,						
and evaluation	50.20	38.20	7.57	1.40	...	...
Military construction	12.36	39.05	22.99	12.86	5.57	3.52
Aggregate for investment group	26.33	33.22	20.28	9.59	4.21	0.95
"Fast-money" operation and support accounts						
Military personnel	94.09	5.30	0.03	...	...	...
Operation and maintenance	74.28	19.85	2.65	...	...	...
Family housing	49.44	27.13	12.13	4.64	2.24	1.00
Aggregate for operation and support group[a]	82.87	13.31	1.64	0.10	0.05	0.02

Source: Department of Defense, *Financial Summary Tables, Department of Defense Budget for Fiscal Years 1988 and 1989* (DOD, 1987), tabs A, O. Aggregate outlay rates are developed using the procedure set forth in Joshua M. Epstein, *The 1987 Defense Budget* (Brookings, 1986), appendix.
a. If OMB's "other" category is included (see *Historical Tables*), and the military personnel outlay rate is applied, the rates in this row become 83.08, 13.16, 1.61, 0.10, 0.05, and 0.02.

Table 6. Defense Outlays If Budget Authority Were Zero for Fiscal Years 1988–92
Millions of dollars unless otherwise specified

Appropriation title	1988	1989	1990	1991	1992	Five-year total
Investment						
Procurement	70,175	42,654	18,695	6,555	1,065	139,144
Research, development, test,						
and evaluation	17,011	3,251	514	0	0	20,776
Military construction	4,435	2,383	1,180	486	189	8,673
Operation and support						
Military personnel	3,953	22	0	0	0	3,975
Operation and maintenance	17,800	2,111	0	0	0	19,911
Family housing	1,408	600	237	98	31	2,374
Other	415	96	25	0	0	536
Energy	3,511	668	105	0	0	4,284
Total	118,708	51,785	20,756	7,139	1,285	199,673
Investment as percent of total	77.2	93.2	98.2	98.6	97.6	84.4

Sources: Computed using budget authority data for fiscal 1983–87 from OMB, *Historical Tables, Fiscal Year 1988*, table 5.1, and outlay rates from Department of Defense, *Financial Summary Tables, Fiscal Years 1988 and 1989*, tab O. Each entry is obtained by applying to each appropriation title its outlay rates beginning in 1983 (the earliest year with an outlay impact on 1988) and letting the budget authority spend out, holding budget authority at zero from fiscal 1988 forward. Figures are for 050 and are rounded.

Table 7. The Overall Defense Budget Backlog, Fiscal Years 1988–92
Billions of dollars unless otherwise specified

Item	1988	1989	1990	1991	1992
Total outlays for year[a]	289.3	303.7	321.0	340.0	361.0
Outlays from current-year budget authority[b]	175.9	187.5	199.5	211.6	224.2
Outlays from prior-year budget authority[c]	113.4	116.2	121.5	128.4	136.8
Outlays from prior-year budget authority as percent of year's total outlays	39.2	38.3	37.9	37.8	37.9

a. These are defense budget outlays (051 account) estimated by OMB, *Historical Tables, Fiscal Year 1988*, pp. 3.3(4), 3.3(5).
b. Computed by multiplying each year's budget authority by the first-year aggregate spendout rate (the sum of the first year's spending for each appropriation title, divided by total budget authority found in OMB, *Historical Tables, Fiscal Year 1988*, pp. 5.1[2], 5.1[3]). This rate equals 0.58 for 1988 and, for simplicity's sake, is assumed to maintain that value through 1992. See appendix of Epstein, *The 1987 Defense Budget*, for a fuller discussion of aggregate outlay rates and their use.
c. Total outlays for year minus outlays from current-year budget authority.

Of course, in a new fiscal year total outlays will be the sum of all outlays resulting from budget authority granted in previous years, plus the first-year outlay from the new fiscal year's budget authority. The prior-year backlog, therefore, is simply the year's total outlays net of the first-year outlays from new budget authority. The prior-year backlogs implicit in the administration's multiyear plan are estimated in table 7. Again, because of investment decisions taken during the first six years of the administration, the backlog now represents nearly 40 percent of total outlays—a 50 percent increase over its 1981 value of about 26 percent, inherited from the Carter administration.[6]

This backlog is a matter of concern for the following reason. Barring rescissions of budget authority from earlier years—which would involve cancellation fees and other legal penalties—these prior-year outlays are locked in. Beyond this uncontrollable 40 percent of each year's outlays another 30 percent or so is needed simply to pay, house, and administer the defense establishment. Thus if large deficit reductions—that is, cuts in actual spending—are to be made in the current year, and the major capital projects, such as new strategic and naval programs, are protected from reductions, readiness—which has grown with the budget as a whole—is bound to suffer badly.

Large new investment programs, such as shipbuilding, should there-

6. The 1981 figure is from William W. Kaufmann, *A Reasonable Defense* (Brookings, 1986), p. 28.

Table 8. Obligation and Outlay Rates for Shipbuilding and Conversion,
Fiscal Years 1988–93
Percent

Item	1988	1989	1990	1991	1992	1993
Obligations[a]	55.40	16.70	6.40	4.40	17.10	. . .
Outlays[b]	5.99	17.00	20.00	21.00	15.00	10.00

Source: Department of Defense, *Financial Summary Tables, Fiscal Years 1988 and 1989*, tab O.
a. Percent of first-year budget authority obligated.
b. Percent of first-year budget authority spent.

fore not be undertaken lightly, since substantial multiyear contractual obligations will result. Money is locked into contract (obligated) long before it is actually spent (outlays), and the relationship is especially acute in the shipbuilding area (table 8).

Overcoming the resultant budgetary momentum is not easy. For example, if because of deficit reduction pressures Congress decided that *outlays* were to be frozen in real or nominal terms, substantial reductions in budget authority would be required. For example, assuming the current mix among appropriation titles, more than $300 billion would have to be cut from the administration's five-year budget authority plan to effect a nominal freeze on outlays (table 9). Again, the main contributor to the momentum—the bow wave—is investment spending.

While a nominal freeze on outlays would strike many as draconian, a real freeze on budget authority has considerable appeal on Capitol Hill. But depending on their composition, different real freezes on budget authority would have different implications for the deficit and, in the most general terms, for the defense posture of the United States. Any such freeze instituted by Congress would fall somewhere on the spectrum anchored at one end by an investment-intensive freeze and at the other by an O&S-intensive freeze. As further context—and as congressional reference points—these basic freezes (and one that takes a middle course) are worth a brief review before specific programs are discussed.

Three Generic Freezes

For lack of better terminology, I call the freezes investment intensive, O&S intensive, and across the board. Their respective outlay consequences are estimated in table 10.

Table 9. **Budget Authority Reductions Required to Produce Real and Nominal Outlay Freezes, Fiscal Years 1988–92**
Millions of dollars unless otherwise specified

		Real outlay freeze			Nominal outlay freeze		
Year	Budget authority request[a]	Derived budget authority level[b]	Difference between request and derived level	Resulting real budget authority growth (percent)	Derived budget authority level[b]	Difference between request and derived level	Resulting real budget authority growth (percent)
1988	311,967	304,590	7,377	0.6	281,962	30,005	−6.9
1989	332,364	323,285	9,081	2.5	290,397	41,967	−0.5
1990	353,463	336,398	17,065	0.7	292,080	61,383	−2.7
1991	374,979	349,117	25,862	0.7	294,019	80,960	−2.4
1992	396,907	357,136	39,771	−0.6	292,782	104,125	−3.2
Total reduction needed	. . .	. . .	99,155	. . .	. . .	318,439	. . .

a. See table 3; data are for 050.
b. The budget authority levels needed to make outlays conform to the specified growth tracks are calculated using the equations presented in the appendix of Epstein, *The 1987 Defense Budget,* and the following five-year aggregate outlay rates: 0.58, 0.22, 0.10, 0.04, and 0.02. The computation of these aggregate outlay rates uses outlay rates for each individual appropriation title, from Department of Defense, *Financial Summary Tables, Fiscal Years 1988 and 1989,* tab O. The calculation assumes no rescission of prior-year budget authority and no change in the mix among appropriation titles from the base year forward.

Predictably, a budget authority freeze in which the administration's O&S request is honored and investment is reduced accordingly (the investment-intensive freeze) would net smaller outlay savings in the near term than a budget authority freeze implemented by granting the administration's investment request and cutting operation and support. An across-the-board, or pro rata, freeze would generate outlay savings in between those of the other two.

The traditional preference of the military services in peacetime, a preference shared by the Reagan administration, has been to emphasize investment, expanding or modernizing the force (or both), and giving research and development (R&D) efforts a "head of budgetary steam" to ensure against an uncertain future. The impulse is to "get while the getting is good." "Technology," runs the argument, "is America's strength. In a crunch, people and readiness—the core of the O&S accounts—can be quickly obtained. If freeze we must, the O&S-intensive option is best."

One risk inherent in this approach is that the ability of U.S. military forces to deter aggression may weaken if tomorrow's big-ticket items are funded at the expense of today's combat effectiveness (a function of readiness, skill, sustainability, and other factors largely funded under

Table 10. Savings in Outlays from Alternative Real Freezes on Budget Authority, Fiscal Years 1988–92

Millions of dollars

Item	Investment intensive[a]	Operation and support intensive[b]	Across the board[c]
1988			
Cut in budget authority	8,924	8,924	8,924
Savings in outlays	2,350	7,414	5,176
1989			
Cut in budget authority	18,616	18,616	18,616
Savings in outlays	7,866	16,640	12,760
Two-year total			
Cut in budget authority	27,539	27,539	27,539
Savings in outlays	10,216	24,054	17,936
1990			
Cut in budget authority	29,080	29,080	29,080
Savings in outlays	15,651	26,753	21,854
1991			
Cut in budget authority	40,289	40,289	40,289
Savings in outlays	24,900	37,608	31,984
1992			
Cut in budget authority	52,411	52,411	52,411
Savings in outlays	35,242	49,336	43,093
Five-year total			
Cut in budget authority	149,319	149,319	149,319
Savings in outlays	86,008	137,751	114,867

Sources: Tables 3, 5, 9. Data are for 051.

a. Grant administration's operation and support request; cut investment by amount needed to freeze budget authority.

b. Grant administration's investment request; cut operation and support by amount needed to freeze budget authority.

c. Preserve current mix between investment and operation and support.

O&S). If the world is a volatile place, then perhaps the marginal dollar should be allocated to reduce immediate risk, by emphasizing readiness. Moreover, military modernization itself has called a basic premise of the O&S-intensive school into question: it is *not* clear that both readiness and appropriate people can be obtained quickly in a crisis. High technology requires high skill, and high skill cannot be acquired quickly.[7] Finally, insofar as investment is driven by a desire to hedge against

7. On the topic of technology and manpower, see Martin Binkin, *Military Technology and Defense Manpower* (Brookings, 1986).

uncertainties regarding the future, there may be nonbudgetary ways of moderating them; for instance, through arms control.

In light of these points, some would conclude that a freeze would be better effected by granting the administration's O&S request and cutting investment accordingly (an investment-intensive freeze). Of course, the primary risk of a sustained investment-intensive freeze is that the West's technological lead may narrow.

A third way to freeze, similar to the well-known Gramm-Rudman-Hollings procedure, would be an across-the-board cut preserving the current mix among appropriation titles. Such a method of course would concede that the existing ratio of investment to O&S has been correct, an assumption not all would accept. Across-the-board freezes keep defective programs, "lemons," alive, while underfunding programs that deserve higher priority. Freezes that preserve service shares of the budget are equally suspect, as are most other rigid formulas.

Not only are all such procedures artificial, but any freeze proceeds from the assumption that the existing budget total is the correct one. Secretary of Defense Caspar W. Weinberger is right in admonishing that national security should not be held hostage to the federal deficit. If this were 1938, for example, a freeze would be inappropriate. How much should the United States spend and how should that expenditure be allocated among competing programs? As noted earlier, the only way to engage the question is to elaborate the ends one seeks to achieve and to gauge the adequacy and efficiency of the means available.

The main defense issues confronting Congress are discussed in the rest of this study.[8] Strategic forces are taken up first, then conventional forces, leading to a set of recommended adjustments to the defense budget. Like this year's defense budget request, my alternative budget is constructed on a two-year basis.

Strategic Forces

Until recently, the top-priority long-term goal of American strategic policy was unambiguous: the deterrence of nuclear attack on the United States, by threat of nuclear retaliation. On March 23, 1983, in his famous

---

8. The discussion is somewhat selective. For example, since no major adjustment in the U.S. capability toward South Korea is recommended (or proposed by the administration), no analysis is presented.

Star Wars speech, however, President Ronald Reagan presented a radically different goal: to make nuclear weapons "impotent and obsolete" through the development of strategic defenses.[9] Deterrence would be ultimately replaced by defense.

In deciding the future of the strategic defense initiative (SDI), including the fate of this year's request for a 57 percent increase in funding, it is useful to distinguish between the president's epochal vision—supplanting deterrence with *comprehensive* defense—and the more immediate, but no less controversial, objective of enhancing deterrence by deploying *partial* defenses.

Comprehensive Defense and the Replacement of Deterrence

Four years after the president's speech, basic questions remain unanswered concerning a comprehensive strategic defense (against Soviet ICBMs, bombers, cruise missiles, and submarine-launched ballistic missiles). First, at what price, if any, might such a defense prove feasible?

PRICE AND FEASIBILITY. Using assumptions that, on balance, are favorable to SDI—for instance, no growth in Soviet missile and bomber forces—Barry M. Blechman and Victor A. Utgoff have estimated the total investment and ten-year operating costs of a system to be fully operational in the year 2012, designed "to provide comprehensive defense against Soviet long-range missiles and aircraft, plus [the] option to defend against intermediate-range missiles." Their estimate is $770 billion at 1987 prices, with average annual expenditures of $44 billion during the peak ten years.[10] To place this estimate in perspective, $44 billion, for SDI alone, would exceed this year's entire budget request for research, development, test, and evaluation.

Under the current fiscal constraints, even these very optimistic estimates may constitute a robust deterrent to full congressional support. In reality, it is unlikely that a working system's true costs could be held to such levels. Specifically, the critical assumption of Soviet offensive

9. "Address to the Nation, March 23, 1983," in *Weekly Compilation of Presidential Documents,* vol. 19 (Government Printing Office, 1983), p. 448.

10. Barry M. Blechman and Victor A. Utgoff, *Fiscal and Economic Implications of Strategic Defenses,* SAIS Papers in International Affairs, no. 12 (Boulder, Colo.: Westview Press, 1986), p. 4.

restraint is implausible, especially now that SALT II has been abandoned. In 1985 Secretary of Defense Weinberger stated that "even a probable [Soviet] territorial defense . . . would require us to increase the number of our offensive forces."[11] Faced with an American deployment, the Soviets would have every incentive to do likewise; and the CIA has testified that it is well within their capability to double (to 21,000) their number of deployed warheads by the mid 1990s.[12]

Such expansion might permit the Soviets to overcome the system. But *saturation*—overwhelming (with greater numbers, more concentrated attacks, or higher salvo rates) the system's ability to weed out decoys and destroy targets—is only one possible counter to a strategic defense. *Evasion,* through deployment of fast-burn boosters, is another. The Defense Intelligence Agency has reportedly estimated that the Soviets could deploy such boosters by 1993.[13] *Suppression,* through direct mechanical destruction (with space mines) or blinding of critical components is yet another possible tactic.

In this connection the wisdom of pursuing antisatellite (ASAT) capabilities can be questioned, since the Soviets can be expected to respond in kind, developing ASATs that could jeopardize the critical space-based components of a ballistic missile defense. Indeed, an agreement limiting further development and testing of antisatellite weapons could prove critical to any future space-based defense.[14]

In short, the feasibility and, in turn, the price and affordability of any comprehensive strategic defense system would depend heavily on the adversary; it is unimaginable that either superpower would sit idly by and watch its deterrent be eroded. Lieutenant General James A. Abrahamson, the SDI's director, may have given a more accurate vision of the future when, during House testimony in 1986, he was asked whether

11. Cited in Leslie H. Gelb, "'Star Wars' Advances: The Plan vs. the Reality," *New York Times,* December 15, 1985.

12. Statement of Lawrence K. Gershwin, National Intelligence Officer for Strategic Programs, CIA, *Soviet Strategic Force Developments,* Joint Hearing before the Subcommittee on Strategic and Theater Nuclear Forces of the Senate Committee on Armed Services and the Subcommittee on Defense of the Senate Committee on Appropriations, 99 Cong. 1 sess. (GPO, 1986), p. 14.

13. Fred Kaplan, "Snag Seen for 'Star Wars' Defense," *Boston Globe,* February 3, 1986. See also Blechman and Utgoff, *Fiscal and Economic Implications.*

14. For a comprehensive discussion of the ASAT question, see Paul B. Stares, *Space and National Security* (Brookings, 1987).

he saw "the countermeasure and counter-countermeasure proceeding in the area and sphere of strategic space defense in the same manner we have seen it elsewhere?" He answered, "Yes."[15]

The course of such measure-countermeasure competitions is not predictable. Under certain assumptions, however, not even unlimited expenditures will guarantee an escape from the mutual hostage relationship that has so far characterized the nuclear era. Specifically, in an unconstrained U.S.-Soviet offensive and defensive arms race, each side would attempt to counter the adversary's defense by adding offensive forces, and to counter the other's offense by building defenses (as well as further offenses). Despite the deployment of strategic defenses capable of absorbing thousands of attacking warheads, neither side's security would necessarily improve. Rather, the arms races could cancel each other out, leaving warheads deliverable in first and second strikes literally unchanged. In short, an unfettered offense-defense arms race could amount to a monumentally expensive freeze on deliverable warheads, which of course are the only kind that matter.

DESIRABILITY. Even assuming comprehensive strategic defense to be feasible and affordable, many people question the desirability of a world in which nuclear weapons have been rendered "impotent and obsolete." Would conventional war be more likely in such a world? With remarkable prescience, Winston Churchill foresaw a world of mutual deterrence "where safety will be the sturdy child of terror, and survival the twin brother of annihilation."[16] It is hard to imagine conventional forces alone providing an equivalent to the nuclear terror—and hence, to nuclear deterrence.[17]

In some respects, however, it is only when such issues are swept aside that the most disturbing questions about comprehensive strategic defense arise. Assuming comprehensive strategic defense to be feasible, affordable, and desirable, is it safely attainable? Can the superpowers achieve it without encountering great strategic instability en route? Is a stable transition possible?

15. R. Jeffrey Smith, "Offensive Taken for Partial SDI Deployment," *Washington Post*, January 18, 1987.
16. Speech before the House of Commons on March 1, 1955, *New York Times*, March 2, 1955.
17. Moreover, if the "conventional spin-off" arguments advanced by the supporters of SDI are valid, conventional war in the defense-dominant world might be unprecedentedly destructive. Indeed, if it is destructive enough, one is hard put to see what would be gained by the elimination of deliverable nuclear arms.

THE TRANSITION PROBLEM. A strategic relationship is said to be crisis stable when neither side feels an incentive to preemptively attack the other in a crisis. One necessary condition for crisis stability is the mutual retention of invulnerable assured destruction capabilities, so that neither side can hope to escape unacceptable retaliatory damage by executing a first strike. If either side (or both) can eliminate the adversary's capacity to do socially mortal damage in a second strike, deterrence will be jeopardized, not enhanced.

The possible paths from a world of mutually assured destruction to the defense-dominant world of mutually assured survival are many. But among those characterized by competition—no sharing of defensive technology, no constraints on the deployment of defenses, and no synchronized constraints on or reductions in deliverable offensive capability—all encounter phases of crisis instability, points at which one or both sides develop such first-strike incentives.[18] That is also the problem with certain types of partial defenses, defenses incapable of handling an all-out first strike.

Partial Defense and the Enhancement of Deterrence

One can imagine many systems of less-than-comprehensive defense. But from a stability perspective it is critical to distinguish between a ground-based partial defense designed to protect only selected military installations, such as missile silos, by intercepting Soviet warheads after their reentry into the earth's atmosphere, and a space-based partial defense designed to attrit any Soviet attack, regardless of its targets, by picking off Soviet missiles in their boost phases, long before their destinations could be determined.

It is the latter type of defense that the Reagan administration and some members of Congress are pressing to deploy. The *deployment* of such a system would violate the 1972 Antiballistic Missile (ABM) Treaty. It would be more vulnerable to Soviet countermeasures than would ground-based terminal defenses, which, if sufficiently limited, need not violate the treaty. And of the two sorts of partial defense, the boost-phase intercept is potentially the more destabilizing. A ground-based

18. For stable transitions under highly cooperative regimes, see Jerome Bracken, *Stability, SDI, Air Defense and Deep Cuts* (Alexandria, Va.: Institute for Defense Analyses, 1986). See also Dean Wilkening and others, "Strategic Defenses and First-Strike Stability," *Survival*, vol. 29 (March–April 1987), pp. 137–65.

Table 11. Effectiveness of a Soviet Strategic First Strike, Fiscal Year 1987

| Item | U.S. preattack strategic nuclear forces | | | U.S. strategic forces surviving if attacked on | | | | | |
| | | | | Day-to-day alert | | | Generated alert | | |
	ICBMs[a]	SLBMs[a]	Bombers[b]	ICBMs[c]	SLBMs[d]	Bombers[e]	ICBMs	SLBMs[f]	Bombers[f]
Launchers	1,000	640	353	260	373	106	260	512	282
Warheads	2,289	5,632	4,926	595	3,268	1,478	595	4,506	3,941
Deliverable in second strike	...	...	...	452	2,613	1,079	452	3,604	2,877
Assignment by target type									
Hard strategic[g]	...	...	...	363	...	731	363	...	1,948
Soft strategic	...	...	...	89	385	348	89	1,249	929
Peripheral attack	...	...	...	...	400	...	...	460	...
General purpose forces	...	...	...	...	400	...	...	460	...
Transportation	...	...	...	...	393	...	...	400	...
Power plants	...	...	...	...	100	...	...	100	...
Urban-industrial	...	...	...	...	935[h]	...	...	935[h]	...

Note: ICBM = intercontinental ballistic missile: SLBM = submarine-launched ballistic missile.

a. Launcher data are from *Department of Defense Annual Report, Fiscal Year 1988*, p. 335; and U.S. Joint Chiefs of Staff, *United States Military Posture FY 1988*, p. 33. Warhead data are from International Institute for Strategic Studies, *The Military Balance 1986–1987* (London: IISS, 1986), pp. 200–01.

b. Launcher data are from *Department of Defense Annual Report, Fiscal Year 1988*, p. 337; and JCS, *United States Military Posture FY 1988*, p. 33. Loadings for FB-111s, B-52G penetrators, and B-52H penetrators are from Congressional Budget Office, *Modernizing U.S. Strategic Offensive Forces: The Administration's Program and Alternatives* (GPO, 1983), p. 86; and Norman Black, "Pentagon Plans to Deploy 'Stealth' Cruise Missiles," *Washington Times*, January 7, 1987. Loadings for the B-1Bs and standoff variants are from IISS, *Military Balance 1986–1987*, p. 222.

c. Surviving launchers are computed assuming the Soviet SS-18 mod 4 overall two-shot (cross-targeted) kill probability given in table 12. Surviving warheads are assumed to be distributed across surviving ICBM types according to their preattack proportions. Deliverable warheads are computed as follows: availability × reliability × number surviving = 0.95 × 0.80 × 595 = 452, using the availability figure from CBO, *Modernizing*, p. 84, and the reliability figure from CBO, *Counterforce Issues*, p. 18.

d. Assumes day-to-day alert rates from CBO, *Counterforce Issues*, p. 26, of 55 and 65 percent for Poseidon and Trident, respectively, and generated alert rates of 80 percent for both. A reliability of 80 percent is applied to obtain deliverable warheads. CBO, *Retaliatory Issues for the U.S. Strategic Nuclear Forces* (GPO, 1978), p. 9.

e. For launchers, this analysis uses the 30 percent alert rate given in CBO, *Modernizing*, p. 100. To compute surviving warheads, preattack loadings are multiplied by 0.3, then summed. On deliverable warheads, CBO estimates the compound probability of reliable operation and penetration of Soviet air defenses as between 70 percent and 76 percent; the average, 73 percent, is assumed. CBO, *Retaliatory Issues*, p. 9.

f. For SLBMs and bombers the generated alert rate of 80 percent from CBO, *Counterforce Issues*, pp. 26, 28, is assumed, even though a 95 percent rate is given in CBO, *Modernizing*, pp. 100, 103–04. Surviving and deliverable warheads are computed as above, with 73 percent deliverable for bombers and 80 percent (reliability) deliverable for SLBMs.

g. MX, Minuteman III and IIIA, air-launched cruise missiles (ALCMs), and gravity bombs are assigned to hard targets; Minuteman II, short-range attack missiles (SRAMs), and SLBM warheads are allocated to other targets.

h. Two hundred equivalent megatons (EMT) at 0.1 megaton per warhead.

these, roughly 3,600 would be SLBM warheads. According to the CIA, "The Soviets still lack effective means to locate United States ballistic missile submarines at sea. . . . we do *not* believe there is *a realistic possibility* that the Soviets will be able to deploy in the 1990s a system that could pose *any significant threat* to United States SSBN's [nuclear ballistic missile submarines] on patrol."[21]

The window narrows further when one considers that the United States could—technically—launch its ICBMs on warning of a Soviet attack, adding roughly 1,800 warheads to the retaliatory blow suffered by the USSR.[22] Though launch-on-warning is an extremely hazardous doctrine, no prudent Soviet planner can ignore the possibility. This uncertainty contributes to deterrence. Aside from the many uncertainties associated with U.S. operational behavior, the Soviets also face technical uncertainties.[23] Finally, even assuming these are overcome and Soviet ICBMs perform as well as currently estimated (table 12), and that the United States chooses to ride out the Soviet attack, the prevailing assumption that the American ICBM force would be wiped out is simply not supported by the available evidence. Rather, about 26 percent of the launchers and roughly 26 percent of the warheads (more than 500) would survive. This finding, moreover, is consistent with the congressional testimony of CIA officials responsible for the analysis of Soviet capability.[24]

All told, a conservative Soviet planner today would have to bank on an overall American retaliatory capability of some 6,900 warheads. It is difficult to fathom how that deterrent should call for enhancement, either through partial strategic defenses or other means, such as deploying 500

21. Statement of Gershwin, *Soviet Strategic Force Developments*, Hearing, p. 17. Emphasis added.
22. This assumes a reliability of .8. See note c of table 11.
23. See, for example, Bruce W. Bennett, *How to Assess the Survivability of U.S. ICBMs*, R-2577-FF (Santa Monica, Calif.: Rand Corp., 1980).
24. "The Soviet capability today against Minuteman silos is substantial but not perfect by any means. . . . It is certainly not our intention to create the impression that the Soviets today could destroy all Minuteman silos, period. They could do a pretty good job against them." Lawrence K. Gershwin, quoted in Michael R. Gordon, "CIA Downgrades Estimate of Soviet SS-19 . . . Saying Missile Too Inaccurate for First Strike," *National Journal*, vol. 17 (July 20, 1985), p. 1693. More recently, the Department of Defense itself has estimated that "20 percent to 35 percent of the silos would survive" an attack by SS-18 mod 4 missiles. Congressional Budget Office, *Trident II Missiles: Capability, Costs, and Alternatives* (GPO, 1986), p. 15. Further details can be found in Department of Defense, *Soviet Military Power, 1986*, 5th ed. (GPO, 1986), p. 25.

Table 12. Assumed Soviet ICBM Performance in Two-on-One Attacks against U.S. Silos of 2,000-Psi Hardness[a]

Soviet ICBM	Accuracy of attacking warhead (CEP, in nautical miles)[b]	Explosive yield (megatons)[c]	Overall two-shot kill probability[d]
SS-18 mod 4	0.135	0.50	0.74
SS-19 mod 3	0.150	0.55	0.70
1985 CIA reestimate	0.216	0.55	0.46

a. Assumes Soviets allocate two warheads per U.S. silo. U.S. silo hardness of 2,000 pounds per square inch (psi) is from CBO, *Modernizing*, p. 84.

b. Circular error probable (CEP) is the radius of a circle within which the warhead has a 50 percent probability of landing. CEP for the SS-18 mod 4 is from IISS, *The Military Balance 1985–1986*, p. 162; for the SS-19 mod 3, I assume the SS-19 follow-on estimate from CBO, *Modernizing*, p. 90; this imputes to the SS-19 mod 3 higher accuracy than is given it specifically (0.162 nautical miles) in IISS, *Military Balance 1985–1986*, p. 162. The CIA reestimated the SS-19 mod 3's accuracy downward in 1985. The figure is from Michael R. Gordon, "CIA Downgrades Estimate of SS-19 . . . Saying Missile Too Inaccurate for First Strike," *National Journal*, vol. 17 (July 20, 1985), p. 1692.

c. Yields are from IISS, *Military Balance 1985–1986*, p. 181.

d. Computed as $1 - (1 - TPK)^2$, where the terminal kill probability, TPK, equals the product of a weapon's reliability and single-shot kill probability, $SSPK$. $SSPK = 1 - 0.5^{(LR/CEP)^2}$, where the lethal radius, LR, is computed as a function of warhead yield and target hardness using the first formula given by Lynn Etheridge Davis and Warner R. Schilling, "All You Ever Wanted to Know about MIRV and ICBM Calculations but Were Not Cleared to Ask," *Journal of Conflict Resolution*, vol. 17 (June 1973), p. 213. The algorithm credits the Soviets with perfect cross-targeting so that reliability is maximized over the attack. Overall reliabilities of 80 percent are assumed, higher than the value of 75 percent given in CBO, *Counterforce Issues*, p. 16.

of the single-warhead mobile ICBMs known as Midgetman, a weapon that gained bipartisan support when proposed by the President's Commission on Strategic Forces (the Scowcroft Commission) in 1983.[25]

Given existing and programmed (see discussion below) U.S. retaliatory capabilities, the stability arguments for Midgetman ring hollow. It is hard to believe that the Soviets' inclination to launch a first strike against the United States would be at all sensitive to the addition of 500 more ICBM warheads to the U.S. inventory. Nor (regarding single- versus multiple-warhead missiles) is it clear why the Soviets would be perceptibly *more tempted* to attack the same marginal 500 warheads if they were deployed on 50 MX missiles (at 10 warheads apiece) *than if* they were deployed on 500 single-warhead Midgetman missiles. Why should the Soviets be tempted to attack either force, or for that matter, current forces? Before the United States spends $45 billion on Midgetman, these questions and others raised below deserve serious answers. For example, Midgetman missiles will have excellent hard-target kill capabilities; why is it ''stabilizing'' for the United States to procure any more counterforce weaponry than is already programmed?

25. *Report of the President's Commission on Strategic Forces* [The Scowcroft Commission], April 1983, pp. 15–16.

Table 13. Programmed U.S. First- and Second-Strike Prompt Hard-Target Kill Capability, with No Midgetman and 50 MX Missiles

		First strike		Second strike	
System	Two-shot kill probability	Maximum number of targets attacked	Expected targets destroyed	Maximun number of targets attacked	Expected targets destroyed
Trident II Mark 5	0.86	2,400	2,064	1,920	1,651
1 MX plus 1					
MMIIIA[a]	0.86	500	430	130	112
Total	. . .	. . .	2,494	. . .	1,763

Source: CBO, *Trident II Missiles*, pp. 10, 51-3, and table 11. CBO assumes Soviet targets of 5,000 psi hardness, U.S. missile reliabilities of .8, and single-shot kill probabilities of 79 percent for Trident II Mark 5, 93 percent for MX, and 57 percent for MMIIIA.
a. Minuteman III Mark 12A.

THE SOVIET WINDOW OF VULNERABILITY. Indeed, not only are U.S. second-strike capabilities programmed to grow, but—with the planned deployment of 50 MX and 20 Trident submarines, equipped with Trident II missiles—the United States will acquire a much better first-strike capability against Soviet ICBMs (which hold over 60 percent of Soviet warheads) than the Soviets have ever had against U.S. ICBMs (which account for only about 20 percent of U.S. warheads).

According to the Congressional Budget Office, "by the year 2000 when 20 Trident submarines would be deployed under the Administration's plan, the U.S. inventory of hard-target warheads on ballistic missiles would have grown to approximately 6,800, including 4,800 warheads on Trident II SLBMs, and at least 500 warheads on MX ICBMs."[26] From the current U.S. inventory of 1,650 hard-target warheads—all of them far less capable than Trident IIs—deployed on ballistic missiles, this represents a literal quadrupling. It "would transform the ability of the United States to conduct large-scale attacks on hardened targets in the Soviet Union."[27] Against the very hardest of Soviet targets, such as ICBM silos, the U.S. force will have the imposing first- and second-strike capabilities shown in table 13.

Clearly, all the Soviets' current 1,398 ICBM silos would be at extreme risk, which is one reason why the Soviets are moving to mobile missiles (and is also why the American offer of November 1985 at the Geneva conference to ban mobile missiles was not universally regarded as

26. Congressional Budget Office, *Trident II Missiles*, p. 4.
27. Ibid., p. xi.

realistic). Indeed, the number of fixed Soviet silos is projected to fall to about 900 by the time the Trident program is complete.

If the Soviets are evacuating fixed silos in favor of mobility, why should the U.S. invest heavily in weapons—such as Midgetman and further MX missiles—that are optimized only against *fixed* hard targets, especially when that (shrinking) target set will already be well covered? Indeed, without any Midgetman missiles, and holding the MX force to 50, the U.S. capability against Soviet ICBM silos and hardened strategic command and control bunkers will make the American "window of vulnerability" look rather modest. This leaves aside the first-strike potential inherent in the Pershing II missile force.

Moreover, though it is seldom noted, stealth weaponry (the advanced technology bomber and advanced cruise missile) may also pose a first-strike threat, and not merely because of yield and high accuracy, though the combination promises to be potent. Rather, there is a widespread, and questionable, presumption that the only first-strike weapons are the fast-flying, "prompt," hard-target killers, the ballistic missiles. Speaking precisely, however, it is not their short flight times (their literal promptness) that make ballistic missiles first-strike counterforce weapons. Rather, it is the limited reaction time their speedy delivery would afford the Soviets. In practice, however, an undetected attack by slow-flying stealth cruise missiles (and bombers) could give the Soviets even less reaction time than an attack by faster flying, but more easily detected, ballistic missiles. (For this reason, a ban on all ballistic missiles, as proposed in 1986 at the U.S.-Soviet summit meeting in Reykjavik, might not, in fact, increase stability, since in a world of stealth cruise missiles, reciprocal fears of surprise attack might actually grow!)

In any event, the advocates of the $45 billion Midgetman ICBM, and of further MX missiles, have yet to make a case that the United States needs prompt first- or second-strike hard-target kill capabilities beyond those to be provided by the Trident IIs, 50 MXs, and the Minuteman IIIA force. Some would hold that the first-strike capabilities programmed are already excessive and potentially destabilizing, or will become so if and when augmented by strategic defenses.

Sometimes an "astrategic" argument for Midgetman is advanced—namely, that because of age the Minuteman ICBM force will require routine replacement in the near future. First, even if it were true that the Minuteman III force required routine replacement, it would not follow that Midgetman specifically would be required, given the alternatives (including a new three-warhead Minuteman). And, in fact, Minuteman does not require routine replacement. At a cost of billions of dollars, the Minuteman's motors and other critical subsystems have been modernized; practically speaking, the Minuteman IIIA is a new missile. Moreover, the 50 Minuteman missiles removed from their silos to make room for the 50 silo-based MX missiles that are planned will permit six to ten years of Minuteman reliability testing (at eight firings a year in the first case and five in the second), to ensure that the force stays in top condition.

SURVIVABILITY OF MOBILE MISSILES WITHOUT SALT II. Not only would mobile Midgetmen and rail-mobile MX be unnecessary as routine replacements, and superfluous from a target-coverage standpoint, if not outright destabilizing, but their survivability itself is dubious. Unconstrained by SALT II, or comparable limits on strategic offensive forces, the Soviets, according to the CIA, could increase their strategic warheads from the current total of about 10,000 to between 16,000 and 21,000 by the mid-1990s. Even the higher number, the CIA says, "is not a maximum effort," which could bring the total to nearly 28,000.[28]

At such levels of Soviet strategic offense, schemes to enhance ICBM survivability by deploying them on mobile launchers are unlikely to succeed. As shown in table 14, the Soviets would be able to (1) barrage a force of 500 Midgetman missiles dispersed, on hard mobile launchers, over the 17,000 square nautical miles of southwestern territory owned by the Departments of Defense and Energy; (2) barrage a force of 50 MX missiles deployed as contemplated on 18,250 miles of commercial railroad track; (3) cover 1,000 ICBM silos at two warheads per silo; and (4) accomplish a broad spectrum of further countermilitary tasks, while withholding all the warheads required to promptly obliterate over 50 percent of America's urban population.[29] By contrast, if the Soviets were constrained to levels of strategic offense permitted under SALT II, they would fall short of those targeting goals by more than 6,000 warheads.

28. The CIA data and quotation are from Gershwin, *Soviet Strategic Force Developments*, Hearing, p. 14. The figure of 28,000 is a Congressional Research Service estimate of a "rapid expansion" but not a "crash program." See Al Tinajero and others, *U.S./Soviet Strategic Nuclear Forces: Potential Trends with or without SALT*, Library of Congress, Congressional Research Service, Report 84-174 F (CRS, 1984), pp. 24, 34.

29. This calculation is optimistic, moreover, in assuming that the rail-mobile MX is not caught in its garrisons by a bolt-from-the-blue attack. Far fewer Soviet warheads would be required to destroy the force in its garrisons.

Table 14. Mid-1990s Soviet Warhead Demand and Supply with and without SALT II Limits

Mission	Number	Warheads per target	Delivered warheads required
90 percent damage expectancy against rail-mobile MX	. . .	. . .	5,680[a]
90 percent damage expectancy against area-mobile small ICBM (Midgetman)	. . .	. . .	7,650
Cross-target 1,000 ICBM silos at 2:1	. . .	. . .	2,000
Subtotal	. . .	. . .	**15,330**
Cover Strategic Air Command (SAC) bomber and tanker bases	34	15	510
Cover nuclear Navy bases	16	2	32
Cover nuclear weapons storage facilities	9	2	18
Cover missile launch control centers	100	2	200
Cover national command posts and alternative headquarters	7	1 + 1(at 5)	12
Cover early warning radars	5	1	5
Cover Navy radio transmitters	10	1	10
Cover SAC radio transmitters	9	1 + 1(at 2)	11
Cover satellite command transmitters	9	1	9
Subtotal[b]	. . .	. . .	**807**
Deliver 200 equivalent megatons (at 0.5 megaton per warhead)	. . .	. . .	**317**
Total warheads delivered	. . .	. . .	**16,454**
Peacetime demand (at overall reliability of 0.8)	. . .	. . .	20,568
Peacetime supply (without SALT and maximum rates)[c]	. . .	. . .	27,798[d]
Peacetime supply (with SALT limits)[c]	. . .	. . .	14,214[e]

a. Barrage requirements for rail-mobile MX and area-mobile Midgetman are derived as follows. For MX, a line barrage is required. The number of warheads, N, required to barrage a line of distance, d, with a packing factor of f and damage expectancy of D is given by $N = dfD / 2R$, where R is the lethal radius of the attacking warheads (expressed in the same units as distance). To barrage an area of A square units, with f, d, D, and R as defined above, $N = AfD / \pi R^2$.

For targets of hardness p (psi), the lethal radius R (in meters) of a weapon of yield Y_{KT}, detonated at its *optimal* height of burst, is (in meters):

$$R(Y_{KT})_m = Y_{KT}^{1/3} \cdot \begin{cases} 2224\,p^{-.744} & \text{if } 1 \le p < 10 \\ 1685\,p^{-.620} & \text{if } 10 \le p < 100 \\ 384\,p^{-.296} & \text{if } 100 \le p < 10,000 \\ 318\,p^{-.273} & \text{if } p \ge 10,000 \end{cases}$$

This formula was obtained by curve fitting the overpressure results of Harold L. Brode and Stephen J. Speicher, *Air Blast from Nuclear Bursts—Analytic Approximations,* prepared for the Defense Nuclear Agency (Los Angeles: Pacific-Sierra Research Corp., 1985).

The results in the table are obtained assuming 500 KT Soviet warheads, damage expectancies of 90 percent, packing factors of 1.2, hardnesses of 30 psi for Midgetman and 12.5 psi for MX, 17,000 square nautical miles as the deployment area for Midgetman, and 18,250 miles as the rail distance for MX. The last value is from General Accounting Office, *ICBM Modernization: Status, Survivable Basing Issues, and Need to Reestablish a National Consensus,* GAO NSIAD-86-200 (GAO, 1986), p. 53. The use of 12.5 psi for rail-mobile MX is assumed to be favorable to the system based on the survivability record given in Samuel Glasstone and Philip T. Dolan, eds., *The Effects of Nuclear Weapons,* 3d ed. (Department of Defense and Department of Energy, 1977), pp. 192–93.

b. The source for this group is William Daugherty, Barbara Levi, and Frank von Hippel, "The Consequences of 'Limited' Nuclear Attacks on the United States," *International Security,* vol. 10 (Spring 1986), p. 30.

c. Soviet capacities are from Al Tinajero and others, *U.S./Soviet Strategic Nuclear Forces: Potential Trends with or without SALT,* Library of Congress, Congressional Research Service, Report 84-174F (CRS, 1984), p. xii.

d. 7,230 surplus.

e. 6,354 deficit.

Here the policies of the Reagan administration conflict. It has abandoned SALT II, removing all constraints on Soviet offensive force levels, but is planning to deploy mobile ICBMs whose survival requires precisely that Soviet offensive forces be capped.

In fact, without arms control, mobile missiles play to the Soviets' strength: sheer quantitative force growth. The superhardening of U.S. silos would at least require that the Soviets improve their force qualitatively, by greatly increasing its accuracy. All else fixed, to achieve against 50,000 psi silos the same two-shot kill probability of 74 percent they now enjoy against 2,000 psi silos, the Soviets' accuracy (SS-18 mod 4) would have to triple (that is, fall from 0.135 naut. mi. CEP [circular error probable] to 0.045 naut. mi. CEP). This would pose a real technological challenge to the Russians and could prolong the life of the U.S. ICBM force.[30]

Clearly, hardening silos is not the only alternative to Midgetman, or rail-mobile MX missiles, as a way to enhance deterrence *if* that is deemed essential. Other possibilities are deep underground basing of ICBMs plus upgraded command and control to submarines (if necessary), increases in submarine force levels, or further procurement of sea- or air-launched cruise missiles. The last of these bears on the future of the bomber.

MANNED BOMBERS. The basic question here is sometimes forgotten. In how many ways must the United States be able to penetrate Soviet air defenses with bombers and cruise missiles? The B-52 bomber (which is further equipped with its own nuclear-armed defense-suppression

---

30. If superhardening were combined with deceptive basing—multiple empty silos for each full one—even more time could be purchased. If the only goal of Midgetman, moreover, is to raise the Russians' "price to attack" (in warheads expended in an attack), there are other ways to do it without buying more counterforce capability. For instance, it has not been shown that deceptive basing, combined with preferential terminal defense, would not exact comparable prices. On such defenses, Kenneth Flamm and I have proved the following theorem. Let W be the minimum number of (perfect) warheads an attacker must send against an M-missile complex preferentially defended by D (perfect) interceptors in order to be certain that no more than S missiles survive. Then

$$W = \left(\frac{D}{S+1} + 1 \right) M.$$

If there are F fake (that is, empty) silos, in addition to M full ones,

$$W = \left(\frac{D}{S+1} + 1 \right) (M + F).$$

missile) can penetrate Soviet air defenses through corridors cut for it by submarine-launched ballistic missiles. Using the same tactic, or using its low radar profile, active electronic countermeasures, and nuclear short-range attack missile to shoot its way in, the B-1 bomber will provide higher confidence of penetration. Air-launched cruise missiles released by B-52s (or B-1s) from outside of Soviet airspace, or cruise missiles launched from sea (the nuclear Tomahawk land-attack missile, TLAM/ N), provide yet other, very high confidence means of nuclear strike. In fact, in the CIA's estimation, "against a combined attack of penetrating bombers and cruise missiles, Soviet air defenses during the next 10 years probably would not be capable of inflicting sufficient losses to prevent large-scale damage to the USSR."[31]

Looking to the future, the application of stealth technology to cruise missiles, as envisioned in the advanced cruise missile (ACM) program, promises to increase further the already high confidence the United States enjoys. But though stealth technology, applied to cruise missiles and importantly to conventional forces, deserves strong support, the case for the stealth manned penetrating strategic bomber (also called the ATB, for advanced technology bomber) has yet to be made, given the existing means of penetrating Soviet airspace, and particularly given the stealth bomber's projected costs, which have been estimated to total nearly $26 billion for 1983 through 1990.[32]

Conclusions

Although the theoretical vulnerability of America's land-based ICBM force is a matter of long-term concern, there is time to bring U.S. arms

31. Statement of Gershwin, *Soviet Strategic Force Developments*, Hearing, p. 17.

32. Estimate from Joseph F. Campbell, "Stealth Bomber: Program on Track, Growth for Northrop," Paine Webber Status Report, February 13, 1986, p. 3. Campbell's figure is $25,905 million for 1983–90. Moreover, even if, having driven the Soviets out of fixed silos, the United States now wishes to chase down and attack their mobile ICBMs as they roam the Russian steppe, it still does not follow that the stealth bomber is necessarily the appropriate weapon system. Will it have the range, payload, and reliability to do the job? Ironically, the B-1's well-publicized problems (see note 2), like some other procurement "horror stories," are at least partly the result of the emergency mentality produced by an exaggerated threat assessment. "We're in desperate straits; get everything yesterday. Don't worry about concurrency or production cost." Since the United States can penetrate Soviet airspace in a variety of ways, it can surely afford to subject the stealth bomber to greater scrutiny, ensuring at least that if a legitimate mission for manned penetrators is identified, the United States will have a plane that can reliably execute it.

Table 15. **Proposed Alterations to the Administration's Strategic Nuclear Plan, Fiscal Years 1988–89**
Billions of dollars

Program	Action	Budget authority (050) savings 1988	Budget authority (050) savings 1989
Small ICBM (Midgetman)	Cancel	2.3	2.3
MX missile	Cap at 50; reduce test procurement for 50 deployed; eschew rail-mobile option	0.9	1.6
Strategic defense initiative (DOD)	Freeze at fiscal 1986 level	2.5	3.5
Strategic defense initiative (DOE)	Freeze at fiscal 1986 level	0.2	0.0
Antisatellite (ASAT) program	Cancel	0.4	0.8
Advanced technology bomber (ATB)	Hold in reduced development	2.0	2.0
Total savings in budget authority	. . .	8.3	10.2
Resulting savings in outlays	. . .	(2.2)	(5.4)

Sources: Department of Defense, *Program Acquisition Costs by Weapon System, Fiscal Years 1988 and 1989*, pp. 78, 83, 136, 148, and *Fiscal Year 1987*, p. 177; Center on Budget and Policy Priorities, Defense Budget Project, "Factsheet on the Strategic Defense Initiative Budget," January 14, 1987, Congressional Budget Office, "The MX Missile Test Program and Alternatives," staff working paper (February 1986); and Federation of American Scientists.

control policies and strategic modernization programs into sync, to make reasoned choices among the many competing modernization alternatives, and to set a balanced and stabilizing course for the rest of the century at least. Because of the special dynamics of defense spending that were noted at the outset, and the way in which budgetary (and hence, political) momentum can build, the first step is to avoid getting locked into programs—especially defensive ones—before their necessity and efficiency have been established. The adjustments proposed in table 15 reflect that view.

The Midgetman missile would be cancelled and the deployed MX force capped at 50. Rail-mobile basing for MX would be eschewed. Growth rates in funding for SDI and the stealth bomber would be reduced and new funding for antisatellite weaponry denied.

For the strategic forces, the essential question is whether the enhancement of deterrence is an urgent matter calling for the rapid and simultaneous modernization of all legs of the strategic offensive triad—including two new bombers, two new ICBMs, both stealth and nonstealth cruise missiles, new Trident submarines and Trident II hard-target killing missiles—plus vigorous prosecution of ASAT capabilities and the earliest possible deployment of a partial boost-phase defense that would violate the ABM Treaty, the SALT II accord having already been discarded.

As has been argued, a powerful case can be made that the answer is no, that deterrence is robust, and that, given the existing means of performing basic tasks, some of the administration's programs—duplicative air breathing systems and mobile ICBMs—are superfluous. Moreover, even if the enhancement of deterrence were urgent, it would not follow that the administration's policies constitute either the most economically efficient or politically prudent way to enhance it.

Conventional Forces

The most plausible paths to nuclear war begin with a failure of conventional defenses. For that reason, and because nonnuclear forces account for roughly 80 percent of the defense budget, conventional requirements must be assessed rigorously, by methods that go beyond the side-by-side comparison of peacetime inventories to capture the technological, geographic, and operational factors that often matter most. Nowhere has the failure to appreciate such factors been more systematic, or proved more pernicious, than in the Persian Gulf.

The Persian Gulf

The Soviet military threat to this region has been a prime security concern of the United States since the 1940s. Since the fall of the shah and the invasion of Afghanistan, the Soviet threat to Iran specifically has been the basis for America's rapid deployment force planning. This contingency accounts for the bulk of U.S. defense spending on Southwest Asia: the case for creating a new unified command—U.S. Central Command—and for the Reagan administration's plans to vastly expand the force were both couched primarily in terms of the Soviet threat.[33]

Most recently, of course, President Reagan and other administration officials have sought to justify their secret arms deal with Iran by reference to the Soviet threat. In December 1986 former national security

---

33. The Carter administration created the Rapid Deployment Joint Task Force (RDJTF) in 1980 to strengthen America's military posture in the Gulf. On January 1, 1983, the RDJTF was upgraded and converted to a new unified command, the U.S. Central Command (CENTCOM). At the time the force comprised about 220,000 personnel. That figure, and the Reagan administration's plans for a force totaling 440,000 personnel, are set forth in Congressional Budget Office, *Rapid Deployment Forces: Policy and Budgetary Implications* (CBO, 1983), p. xv.

adviser Robert McFarlane called a Soviet invasion of Iran "more than conceivable if you have examined Soviet exercises conducted in recent years."[34]

In short, the specter of Russian divisions plunging south for the warm water ports and oil fields of the Persian Gulf has been central in shaping the administration's policy toward the region, including its secret arms deals with Iran. The administration, however, has badly exaggerated the Soviet threat to that country.

Because of Iran's forbidding terrain, and the vast distances and limited transportation system between Russia and the Gulf, a Soviet invasion would be fraught with serious vulnerabilities. Remarkably, these vulnerabilities have been explicitly recognized in formerly top-secret planning documents of the U.S. Joint Chiefs of Staff and in an invasion plan written by the Soviet General Staff itself.

If these vulnerabilities were exploited, an American rapid deployment force considerably smaller than that approved by the Reagan administration could mount a successful conventional defense and present an imposing deterrent to Soviet aggression. Units beyond those needed to defend the Persian Gulf could be reallocated to NATO, where ground forces deserve greater attention, naval and air forces having been the main beneficiaries of the Reagan buildup.

To gauge requirements in the Persian Gulf, certain operational realities must be appreciated. Terrain is first among these. Two formidable mountain ranges stand between the USSR and Iran's oil fields: the Elburz mountains in the north and the Zagros mountains further south (figure 3). By road, the distance from Soviet bases to the oil is more than 1,000 kilometers. The transportation system over these mountains is exceedingly limited—a dozen arteries over the Elburz, narrowing to six over the Zagros, including one railroad. This sparse system is dotted with severe choke points, places where the destruction of bridges or tunnels would bring entire Soviet columns to a standstill.

All these facts are well known to American and Soviet military planners, and have been for decades. For instance, the Soviets' own *Command Study of Iran* repeatedly notes "narrow gorges which can be easily blocked."[35] Similarly, in once top-secret studies the American

34. Michael R. Gordon, "1980 Soviet Test: How to Invade Iran," *New York Times,* December 15, 1986.

35. Gerold Guensberg, trans., *Soviet Command Study of Iran* (Moscow, 1941), p. 220.

Figure 3. Iran

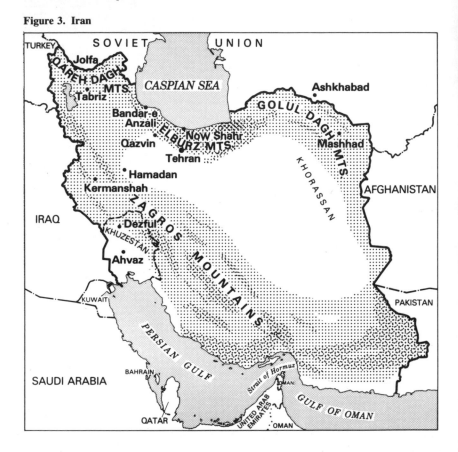

military concluded that "Soviet offensive forces will be limited by their dependence on long overland lines of communication readily harassed by guerrilla or commando type operations and *ideally suited to interdiction* by Allied air."[36]

My own estimate, based on detailed calculations,[37] is that two wings of F-111s (one of the types of aircraft that bombed Libya) could create four to six serious choke points on each of the arteries (road and rail) from the USSR to Tehran in one day of high-intensity flying. This would impose considerable delay on a Soviet drive for oil.

36. Joint Strategic Plans Group, "Proposed Guidance for an Alternative Plan to 'Bushwacker,'" March 8, 1948, p. 130. Emphasis added.

37. See Joshua M. Epstein, *Strategy and Force Planning: The Case of the Persian Gulf* (Brookings, 1987), pp. 107–11.

U.S. special operations forces working in the southern, Zagros, mountains could further attrit and delay the Soviets' advance south. Regarding the countless gorges through the Zagros, the Soviets themselves wrote, "with the use of obstacles or roadblocks these can be turned into excellent defensive positions," a view in which Pentagon planners (in a 1979 study) entirely concurred.[38]

The point of these operations would again be to delay and wear down a Soviet invasion long enough to insert an adequate defensive force in the oil region of the south. What is an adequate force? Detailed analyses of ground combat dynamics indicate that a force of 5 U.S. divisions plus 6 wings of close air support is adequate to contend with the force the Soviets could sustain (logistically) in combat this far from their border.[39]

A force of that size is more efficient than the force of $7\frac{1}{3}$ divisions approved by the Reagan administration, the main difference being the presence in the second case of two superfluous light divisions. The highest U.S. priority should be to increase the speed of the force, through increased sealift, not its size. Any U.S. response timely enough to make $7\frac{1}{3}$ divisions effective is timely enough to make 5 divisions sufficient.[40]

Two of the Army light divisions available to the U.S. Central Command (roughly 10,000 men each) should be disbanded; the personnel should be retained and reorganized as two independent brigades outfitted with tanks (for example, M60A3s) and other stockpiled heavy equipment appropriate for armored warfare in Europe. In the event of war, these brigades could be rounded out with existing National Guard or Reserve forces to form an additional division equivalent for NATO.[41]

These recommendations—which include increased fast sealift over acquisition of the C-17 aircraft—are among the conventional force adjustments set forth in table 20. While increasing the efficiency of the U.S. conventional deterrent in the Persian Gulf, these changes would also enhance NATO's strength.

---

38. Guensburg, trans., *Soviet Command Study*, p. 190; and Capt. Henry Leonard and Jeffrey Scott, "Methodology for Estimating Movement Rates of Ground Forces in Mountainous Terrain with and without Defensive Obstacles," p. 4.1.

39. Epstein, *Strategy and Force Planning*, pp. 44–97, and case 2A of appendix D, pp. 126–45.

40. Ibid., pp. 84–85.

41. Savings from the discontinuation of military construction activities associated with the light division at Fort Drum might be used to procure additional fast sealift for this newly created division for NATO.

NATO and the Warsaw Pact

While differing from the administration's plan, my recommendation to disband Gulf-oriented light divisions in favor of a NATO-oriented heavy one stands diametrically opposed to the recent proposals by several prominent Americans to withdraw substantial numbers of U.S. forces from Europe. For example, former national security adviser Zbigniew Brzezinski has suggested withdrawing 100,000 U.S. troops from Europe and converting them to light divisions for an expanded rapid deployment force. *"Manpower withdrawn from Europe should be absorbed into an enlarged Rapid Deployment Force* through the creation of additional light divisions."[42] Not only would this action reduce what is essential (NATO's current force) to expand what is superfluous (the Army's light divisions), but it would probably increase costs (for example, housing and associated military construction in the United States) rather than save money. Of course, a hope is that the allies would fill the gap. But, as a political signal, it risks the counterproductive result of concern to General Bernard W. Rogers, NATO's supreme allied commander. "If the U.S. withdraws 100,000 troops from Europe, this won't make the West Europeans do more [in terms of their contributions to NATO; rather, such an action] is going to send the kind of message that will lead [the European NATO members] to start to accommodate to the East. It will be an excuse for the U.K. to pull some of its forces back," an action that might stimulate further imitation in Rogers' view.[43] In short, the Brzezinski proposal would most likely prove expensive and politically counterproductive; more important, it is militarily unsound.

FORCE RATIOS. In central Europe improvements beyond the addition of a division equivalent should be made. The current conventional balance, however, is not as bad as is generally assumed. Unfortunately, in reaction to Reykjavik—where ill-considered and disturbing proposals to rapidly eliminate all strategic offensive nuclear arms were discussed— exaggerated assessments of the conventional threat to Western Europe sprang to the fore. Senator Sam Nunn, Democrat of Georgia and chairman of the Armed Services Committee, stated, "We know that the

42. Cited in statement of Zbigniew Brzezinski before the Senate Armed Services Committee, January 13, 1987, p. 7. Emphasis in the original.
43. Edgar Ulsamer, "The Potential Checkmate in Europe," *Air Force Magazine,* vol. 69 (November 1986), pp. 55–56. Brackets in the original.

Soviets and Warsaw Pact currently enjoy an overwhelming advantage in conventional forces.''[44] When asked whether he believed that the Soviet Union has superior conventional forces in Europe, Assistant Secretary of Defense Richard Perle likewise responded, ''I don't think there's any question about that. The Soviet conventional forces vastly outnumber those of the NATO alliance in virtually every category— tanks, aircraft.''[45] More recently, the proposal to eliminate medium- and short-range ballistic missiles from the European theater has prompted further dire assessments, also based on selected numerical differences between conventional forces of NATO and the Warsaw Pact.[46] (A side-by-side comparison of fully mobilized NATO and Warsaw Pact ground divisions and close air support aircraft is given in table 16.)

First, simply as a matter of consistency, if Pentagon leaders really believed static numerical ratios to be as important as such statements suggest, they would be taking money from aircraft carriers, where the United States already vastly outnumbers the Warsaw Pact (14 to 1), and putting money into tanks, rather than proposing to stretch out the latter in order to increase the former. More important, however, as students of military history have long known, static peacetime force ratios are very poor predictors of wartime performance. The only way in which to gauge rigorously the NATO-Pact conventional balance is through dynamic analyses that take into account warfare's dominant operational, tactical, and technological dimensions. As in the Persian Gulf, a static ''bean count'' alone can be totally misleading.

Though they are no substitute for dynamic analyses (plotted in figures 4 and 5 below), the basic facts of the European situation alone suggest that the conventional wisdom may be unduly pessimistic. For instance, NATO has outspent the Warsaw Pact on defense every year since 1965, and a greater percentage of NATO spending is directed at Europe proper. Roughly 15 percent of Soviet spending is directed at China. The Pact is assumed to be unequivocally superior at the conventional level: NATO puts more money *in,* but the Pact is believed to get more military

44. Sam Nunn, ''The Reykjavik Summit: What Did We Really Agree To?'' speech delivered before the United States Senate, October 17, 1986.

45. Cited in transcript of Richard Perle on ABC's ''Nightline,'' October 15, 1986 (American Broadcasting Companies, 1986), p. 2.

46. Indeed, Richard Nixon and Henry Kissinger offer no conventional force data whatever to support their assertion of a ''huge Soviet conventional superiority.'' Richard M. Nixon and Henry A. Kissinger, ''To Withdraw Missiles We Must Add Conditions,'' *Los Angeles Times,* April 26, 1987.

Table 16. M + 90 Static Conventional Balance between NATO and Warsaw Pact Forces on the Central Front[a]

Force	Division formations[b]	Armored division equivalents[b]	Weighted unit value[c]	Close air forces[d]
NATO				
United States	24	$24\frac{1}{5}$	1,149,258	...
United Kingdom	4	$2\frac{1}{2}$	118,725	...
France	12	$3\frac{4}{5}$	180,462	...
West Germany	14	$10\frac{1}{2}$	498,645	...
Other	7	$4\frac{4}{5}$	227,952	...
Total	61	$45\frac{4}{5}$	2,175,042	1,500
Warsaw Pact				
USSR	90	$60\frac{3}{4}$	2,885,017.5	...
Non-Soviet	30	$20\frac{1}{4}$	961,672.5	...
Total	120	81	3,846,690.0	1,600

a. M + 90 stands for mobilization day plus 90 days.

b. From Andrew Hamilton, "Redressing the Conventional Balance: NATO's Reserve Military Manpower," *International Security*, vol. 10 (Summer 1985), p. 116, citing estimates of William P. Mako, *U.S. Ground Forces and the Defense of Central Europe* (Brookings, 1983). Soviet and non-Soviet Warsaw Pact division formations are assumed to have equal ADE scores.

c. Computed by multiplying armored division equivalents by 47,490, the weighted unit value (WUV) of a standard U.S. armored division. Mako, *U.S. Ground Forces*, p. 114. WUV scores provide a common measure of lethality, or combat power, for U.S. and Soviet ground forces. The method was developed by the U.S. Army.

d. Sum of the phase I and phase II fixed-wing and helicopter close air support aircraft for NATO and the Pact, as estimated by Barry R. Posen, "Measuring the European Conventional Balance: Coping with Complexity in Threat Assessment," *International Security*, vol. 9 (Winter 1984–85), p. 72.

capability *out*. The only premises with which this belief is logically consistent are (1) that the Pact is more efficient than NATO or (2) that the Pact's task (offensive warfare) is inherently easier than NATO's (defensive warfare). There is no convincing evidence to support the first premise, while the evidence against the second is weighty. The great Prussian theorist Clausewitz, for instance, held that "*the defensive form of warfare is intrinsically stronger than the offensive.*"[47]

One advantage NATO enjoys as defender is the opportunity to fight from prepared positions. By contrast, the attacker must come into the open, exposing himself to fire, in order to advance. Another defensive advantage, the opportunity to fight on familiar terrain, can be exploited to force Soviet armor into poor tank country. In this connection General Glenn K. Otis, commander in chief of the U.S. Army in Europe, recently discussed the terrain constraints Soviet divisions would face in some

47. Elsewhere, he calls defense "*the stronger form of waging war.*" Carl von Clausewitz, *On War*, Michael Howard and Peter Paret, eds. and trans. (Princeton University Press, 1976), pp. 358–59. Emphases in the original.

important NATO Corps sectors: "The road and the chokepoint constraints—built-up areas, villages, mountain peaks, even some swamps—must be considered. You can't put divisions into those areas, or even individual weapon systems."[48] "Instant" antitank ditches, terrain modifications, prechambering of bridges, and other low-technology initiatives are recommended here.[49] They can exacerbate such Soviet problems and increase the effectiveness of advanced weaponry by forcing the Soviets to stop, increasing their exposure to defensive fire.

In addition, America's allies are more reliable than the Soviet Union's. Western active-duty units generally receive more training than Warsaw Pact units, and Western training is by and large much more realistic. It draws on more combat experience and the accumulated expertise of militarily skillful friends—Israel, for example. Finally, according to the Joint Chiefs of Staff, NATO enjoys a substantial technological lead in many critical military areas. Last June, for instance, General Charles A. Gabriel, as Air Force chief of staff, stated that the Russians were ten years from having planes comparable to the U.S. F-15 and F-16.[50] Historically, such qualitative factors have loomed larger than mere numbers in determining outcomes.

AERIAL WARFARE. The asymmetry is especially pronounced in air-to-air combat (table 17). In World War II American pilots in the Pacific theater lost only one plane for every ten Japanese planes they downed—

48. Charles D. Odorizzi and Benjamin F. Schemmer, "An Exclusive *AFJ* Interview with General Glenn K. Otis, Commander-in-Chief of the U.S. Army in Europe and Commander of NATO's Central Army Group," *Armed Forces Journal International,* vol. 124 (January 1987), p. 46.

49. "Instant" antitank ditches are segments of plastic pipe buried (at a depth of perhaps seven feet) in peacetime. In crisis, an explodable slurry or other liquid would be pumped in (it could also be pumped out if desired). Wartime detonation "would create an inverted 'V' tank ditch that at its deepest point would be about 12–15 feet, and at its widest point some 40 feet across," a serious obstacle for tanks. "Buried Explosive System Creates Tank Ditches Quickly," *Defense News,* February 17, 1986. A thousand kilometers of instant antitank ditching is estimated to cost $100 million (plus 5 percent a year in operation and support). The simple conversion of graded road shoulders into sharp concrete steps (and the emplacement of road dividers) would frustrate cross-road movement of armored forces. For another $100 million, 500 kilometers of road could be regraded, and so forth. Bridges and roads could be "prechambered" to accept enough charges to create 20,000 to 30,000 craters in war for roughly another $100 million (and 5 percent a year operation and support). On these and other approaches, see John C. F. Tillson IV, "The Forward Defense of Europe," *Military Review,* vol. 61 (May 1981), pp. 66–76.

50. George C. Wilson, "Air Force Chief Denies Soviets Ahead in Space," *Washington Post,* June 18, 1986.

40   *Joshua M. Epstein*

Table 17. Exchange Ratios in Aerial Warfare

Theater	Contestants	Winner	Exchange ratio[a]
Pacific (World War II)	United States; Japan	United States	10 to 1
Korea (1950–53)	United States; North Korea	United States	10 to 1
Vietnam (1965–68)	United States; North Vietnam	United States	2.3 to 1
Vietnam (1970–73)	United States; North Vietnam	United States	12.5 to 1
Middle East (1967)	Israel; Arabs	Israel	20 to 1
Middle East (1973–74)	Israel; Arabs	Israel	40 to 1
Lebanon (1982)	Israel; Syria	Israel	86 to 1[b]

Source: Data given in Joshua M. Epstein, *Measuring Military Power: The Soviet Air Threat to Europe* (Princeton University Press, 1984), pp. 110–12.

a. Loser's planes lost to each one of winner's planes lost.

b. 86 Syrian planes shot down with no Israeli losses.

an exchange ratio of 10:1. In the Middle East wars of 1967 (the Six-Day War) and 1973 (the Yom Kippur War), the Israelis scored ratios of 20:1 and 40:1; in Lebanon in 1982 the ratio was more than 80:1. Technological advantages and differences in pilot skill underlie these disparities. It would be imprudent to assume NATO-Pact ratios at the high end of the spectrum, but it is unduly pessimistic to assume that the Pact's modest numerical edge should somehow nullify NATO's superior, and far more extensive, training and its continuing technological lead.[51]

Moreover, in air warfare, as on the ground, defenders may enjoy inherent advantages.[52] These can be supplemented with traditional, proven low-technology approaches to air defense, including increased sheltering for NATO's aircraft, runway hardening and repair, increased point defenses, improved deception and identification-friend-or-foe (IFF) capabilities, high readiness and sortie rates so fewer aircraft are sitting on the ground, and more flying and simulator hours to ensure greater combat effectiveness when they are in the air.

Exploitation of these approaches (none of which are reduced, and some of which are enhanced, under the budgetary alternatives specified here) should make the Soviet air threat manageable. Indeed, a case can

51. On the historical record, see Joshua M. Epstein, *Measuring Military Power: The Soviet Air Threat to Europe* (Princeton University Press, 1984), pp. 110–12. On the numerical balance, see Congressional Budget Office, *Tactical Combat Forces of the United States Air Force: Issues and Alternatives* (CBO, 1985), pp. 19–21.

52. For example, the defender of a high-priority target knows that the Soviet attacker will be *coming to him*, and can create (with electronics) the equivalent of terrain from behind which to ambush the "exposed" attacker.

be made that, despite important strides since the mid-1960s, the Soviet conventional air threat to Western Europe has been somewhat over-rated.[53]

Under the circumstances, it does not seem sensible to be developing two successors to America's most advanced fighter, the F-15—which, according to General Gabriel, is a decade ahead of Soviet planes—and no successor to the A-10 close air support aircraft designed to counter Soviet armor, with which most decisionmakers purport to be concerned. These priorities seem especially misguided, since the United States already underwrites considerable duplication in air defense.

Consider a typical Soviet fighterbomber. NATO is preparing to kill it once in East Germany by bombing its airbase with F-15Es, F-111s, or conventional ballistic missiles; then NATO will "kill" it a second time in air-to-air combat over West Germany with F-16s or F-15s; then NATO will "kill" it a third time from the ground with Patriot surface-to-air missiles.

All three approaches are necessary. But if one asks any of these three air defense communities whether it assumes any contribution from the others when determining requirements, the answer will probably be no. The result is that the problem is solved three times, not once—or even, to be conservative, one and a half times.

Meanwhile other missions—such as close air support—languish. The adjustments proposed here in funding for the F-15, the F-19 (stealth fighter), the ATF (advanced technology fighter), Patriot, and the helicopter LHX (table 20) are intended to reduce the inefficiency and foster a resurgence of close air support, including the development of a successor to the A-10. Full funding is proposed for the Army's forward area air defense (FAAD) program, which includes the development of a successor to the Sergeant York divisional air defense (DIVAD) system.

GROUND ENGAGEMENTS. As noted earlier, ground defenders historically have enjoyed several tactical advantages; operation from prepared, or even fortified, positions and relative concealment are among them. Where such advantages apply, many claim on the basis of military experience that a competent defender should be able to hold territory even if attacker-to-defender lethality ratios reach 3:1. In the words of a May 1984 NATO Military Committee document, "classical military wisdom suggests that a 3:1 ratio in favor of the offense at the point of

53. See Epstein, *Measuring Military Power.*

attack is necessary to assure a reasonable chance of success.''[54] According to the U.S. Army's 1976 version of its operations field manual, FM 100-5, ''as a rule of thumb, [defending generals] should seek not to be outweighed more than 3:1 in terms of combat power. With very heavy air and field artillery support on favorable terrain, it may be possible to defend at a numerical disadvantage of something like 5:1 for short periods of time.''[55] Similarly, on the Soviet side, the European Security Study report notes that ''the minimum numerical superiority ratio sought by the Pact is about 3 to 1 in both ground and air operations. Doctrinally, however, the ratios to be achieved in local conflict situations are to be higher.''[56] Indeed, according to the Pentagon, the Soviets' large military inventories in part ''reflect the offensive nature of Soviet military doctrine and strategy in that attacking forces are believed to require at least a 5:1 force ratio in anticipation of high losses inherent in offensive operations.''[57]

Even if, in raw firepower, NATO were outweighed to such a degree (and it is not), geographic constraints would most likely prevent the Soviets from amassing local force ratios of such magnitudes. Only so much force can be concentrated on a given sector of battlefront. Recent Army analyses have highlighted these so-called force-to-space constraints, and have led General Otis to cut by half the Soviet force he expects his Army group to engage initially: ''Today that [force] equates to a little less than seven divisions, whereas before, we were looking at that [same force] as a 12-to-14 division front. So 12 to 14 divisions might well be there, but they're not all going to be shooting at once because [of] the terrain and geographic limitations.'' Perhaps this reasoning underlies the general's claim that with ''the total NATO capability available to Central Army Group, the first echelon of the Soviet forces is going to have a whale of a time doing anything to us.''[58]

---

54. Karsten Voigt, rapporteur, ''Draft Interim Report of the Sub-Committee on Conventional Defence in Europe'' (Military Committee of the North Atlantic Assembly, May 1984), p. 8.

55. Department of the Army, *Operations: FM 100-5* (Department of the Army, 1976), p. 5-3.

56. Donald R. Cotter, ''Potential Future Roles for Conventional and Nuclear Forces in Defense of Western Europe,'' in *Strengthening Conventional Deterrence in Europe: Proposals for the 1980s,* Report of the European Security Study (St. Martin's Press, 1983), p. 214.

57. Department of Defense, *Soviet Military Power,* 5th ed., p. 63.

58. Odorizzi, ''Exclusive *AFJ* Interview with General Glenn K. Otis,'' pp. 46–47.

Moreover, even after a major mobilization in which the Soviets' second and third echelons (in the USSR) were included, the Warsaw Pact would still not enjoy lethality ratios as high as those said to be needed for high offensive confidence (table 16).

Giving NATO far less credit than the Army's own planning factors would warrant, dynamic simulations of warfare between these fully mobilized forces indicate that NATO has the material wherewithal to stalemate the Warsaw Pact. The solid and dotted curves of figure 4 simulate two NATO–Warsaw Pact wars, each of which is consistent with the prewar static balance as measured in table 16 (that is, with NATO's initial combat power score at 2.2 million and the Pact's at 3.8 million). The curves simulate—in an abstract but conservative way— the mutual attrition over time of NATO and Warsaw Pact forces, the salient point being that, in each case, NATO comes from behind to stalemate the initially larger Warsaw Pact force.[59]

Although a successful conventional forward defense is plausible today, there is little room to spare. No one, on either side of the Atlantic, should be under any illusions about the effect of a significant withdrawal of U.S. combat power. Simply to illustrate the point, the withdrawal of 100,000 *combat* troops, from the mobilized 24 U.S. division formations assumed above, would represent roughly 6 divisions (at 16,000 troops per division), a 25 percent reduction in the U.S. ground complement, and would result in the conventional outcome simulated in figure 5.[60] Almost all of West Germany would be lost, and NATO forces pummeled into defeat, after about five weeks. NATO would be quickly forced to choose between capitulation and nuclear war.

Assessments showing NATO to be the Pact's equal today will change if NATO allows Soviet military investments to go unanswered or fails to maintain its forces in a state of readiness. Such assessments also assume that NATO would properly respond to warning of a Soviet attack, mobilize in a timely way, and be able to sustain nonnuclear operations.[61]

59. Technically, since the curves cross, NATO "wins" in these simulations. But the absolute levels of attrition are close enough to mutual annihilation to make "stalemate" the more conservative and appropriate term. In neither simulation does NATO lose ground.

60. This reduction roughly equates to the withdrawal of 100,000 U.S. *combat* troops, or 6 divisions (at 16,000 troops per division) plus a number of close air support forces.

61. On NATO's current sustainability, see Joshua M. Epstein, *The 1987 Defense Budget* (Brookings, 1986), pp. 45–47.

Figure 4. The Dynamic Conventional Balance between NATO and Warsaw Pact Forces on the Central Front

Ground lethality
(weighted unit value in millions)

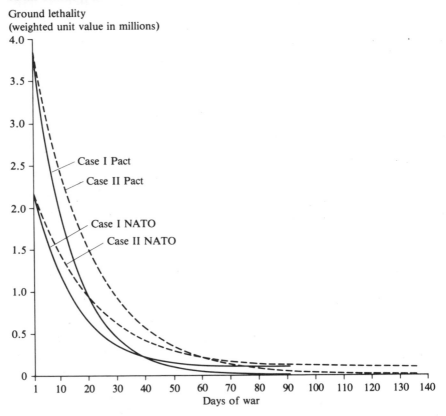

Days of war

Sources: Simulations produced by applying the static numerical estimates of table 16, and other factors, in the dynamic model set forth in Joshua M. Epstein, *The Calculus of Conventional War: Dynamic Analysis without Lanchester Theory* (Brookings, 1985). The other factors employed (see *The Calculus* for complete definitions) are as follows: an average offense-defense ground-to-ground casualty-exchange ratio of 1.85 (far lower than divisional cost ratios and lower than traditional military offense-versus-prepared-defense planning factors of up to 3:1; see Barry R. Posen, "Measuring the European Conventional Balance: Coping with Complexity in Threat Assessment," *International Security*, vol. 9 [Winter 1984–85], pp. 51–52 note, 56, 80–81; and John J. Mearsheimer, "Why the Soviets Can't Win Quickly in Central Europe," *International Security*, vol. 7 [Summer 1982], pp. 15–16); a NATO withdrawal threshold ground attrition rate (in ADEs) of 6 percent a day; a maximum withdrawal rate of 20 kilometers a day (actual withdrawal rates are assumed to depend on the difference between actual attrition rates and the withdrawal threshold rate, here 6 percent); and a Pact equilibrium daily attrition rate of 7.5 percent.

These assumptions conservatively credit the Pact with the capacity to endure attrition rates higher than those NATO is willing to suffer before giving ground (7.5 versus 6 percent). By historical standards, these rates are very high; even so, a fight to the finish lasts three months. For historical rates, see Posen, "Measuring the European Conventional Balance," pp. 79–80. Thirty-three percent reductions in the Pact's equilibrium attrition rate (from 7.5 to 5 percent), in its opening prosecution rate (from 5 to 3.3 percent), and in NATO's withdrawal threshold (from 6 to 4.5 percent) would prolong the war by more than a month, to 136 days, as shown in case II. These are the only assumptions that differ from case I. Each side's close air attrition rate per sortie is 5 percent, high historically; armored fighting vehicles (AFVs) killed per NATO sortie is 0.5, and 0.25 for the Pact; 1,200 AFVs per division equivalent are assumed (see Posen, "Measuring the European Conventional Balance," pp. 72–73). NATO is assumed to average 3 sorties per day; the Pact, 2. For a discussion of comparative Soviet/Western strengths and weaknesses in the ground support of air operations, see Joshua M. Epstein, *Measuring Military Power: The Soviet Air Threat to Europe* (Princeton University Press, 1984), chaps. 2, 3.

Figure 5. Effect of a 25 Percent Reduction in American Force on the NATO–Warsaw Pact Balance

Ground lethality
(weighted unit value in millions)

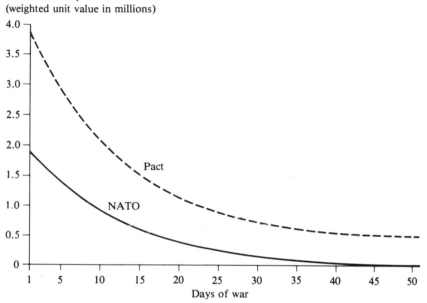

Days of war

Sources: All assumptions are as in figure 4, with the U.S. ADE score and NATO's close air support force reduced by 25 percent.

There is no reason why NATO, history's richest alliance, should fail to meet its requirements and mount an imposing nonnuclear deterrent to conventional attack, especially if all the allies honor their commitments, if a U.S. heavy division equivalent is reallocated from the Gulf to NATO, and if a program of terrain enhancement and obstacle preparation is instituted, as proposed here.

Role of the U.S. Navy

For the Atlantic Alliance to sustain conventional ground and tactical air operations for more than a few months, the U.S. Navy would have to defend NATO's sea line of communication (SLOC) from bombers and submarines of the Soviet Northern Fleet, based at Murmansk on the Kola Peninsula. But this primary naval objective might be achieved in either of two ways: defensively or offensively. The first tactic would have the Navy deploy its aircraft carrier battle groups (CVBGs) near the so-called GIUK (Greenland-Iceland-U.K.) gaps, and lie in wait for the

Soviets, forcing them to run a series of defensive gauntlets before engaging the carriers and Europe-bound convoys. The alternative would be to assemble a large-scale offensive naval strike force and steam north of the GIUK, north of Norway, and around the North Cape to defeat Soviet forces in their home waters. This offensive campaign is a cornerstone of the Navy's maritime strategy, which provides the doctrinal underpinnings for the 15-carrier, 600-ship navy approved by the Reagan administration.

How would a 15-carrier fleet be likely to fare in offensive operations against the Soviet Northern Fleet, given the Navy's stated requirements elsewhere in the world, especially on the assumption—also central to the maritime strategy—of a global war of high intensity, including the option of attacking the Soviet Pacific Fleet (based at Vladivostok and Petropavlovsk)? Specifically, is it plausible that a 15-carrier fleet would succeed in conducting offensive operations in these high-threat areas, as contemplated in the maritime strategy? The answer is no.

To have moderate confidence of success in executing, with aircraft carriers, the offensive missions contemplated in the maritime strategy, the U.S. Navy would need at least a 21-carrier fleet, at ten-year costs exceeding those of the planned 15-carrier fleet by roughly $158 billion. That number is based on an analysis that is explicitly set forth in the note below.[62] Without encumbering the discussion in the text with the technicalities, some of the basic points of the analysis deserve note.

62. The calculation proceeds as follows. The number of carriers required simply to enjoy a reasonable chance of survival against the forces of the Kola complex and supporting air bases depends on (1) the number of direct hits each carrier can suffer before being knocked off station, and (2) the number of carriers required to keep hits per carrier below that level. From Navy curves published in Capt. Stephen T. De La Mater, USN, "The Role of the Carrier in the Control of the Seas," *United States Naval Institute Proceedings,* vol. 98 (May 1972), pp. 110–25, Brian McCue has reconstructed the number of hits, n, needed to achieve a probability, p, of mission kill: $n = \ln(1 - p)/\ln(1 - x)$, where $x = 0.25$ for 90,000 ton carriers. For each carrier to have a 20 percent chance of survival, hits (in integers) must not exceed six; that is the criterion used here. One may check that six expected hits per carrier result if 9 carriers are sent against the Soviet forces shown in table 18, when the attrition rates given there are broken down into two ingress barriers (from within which Soviet munitions are launched) and two egress barriers (through which attackers must escape to return to base for rearming and so forth). For Soviet bombers, the ingress survival probabilities are .8 and .7 and egress are .85 and .9, for the overall full-cycle attrition rate of .57. For Soviet submarines of both types, the corresponding values are .7, .65, .75, and .8, for the full-cycle attrition rate of .73. Soviet forces are simply cycled in and out of these barriers,

Most important, assumptions are simply unavoidable in any analysis. And the assumptions used in the analysis may be wrong. But their accuracy is not the critical issues. Rather, the essential question is whether the assumptions are unfavorable to the Navy. If, as intended, the assumptions favor the Navy, and the mission appears unpromising, then on more accurate (less favorable) assumptions, it can only look *more* unpromising.

MODEL ASSUMPTIONS FORMALLY FAVORABLE TO THE NAVY. Some of those favorable assumptions are implicit in the model, independent of the numbers that are applied in it. For example, the calculation does not permit any degradation in the carrier's defensive performance as hits accumulate. Carrier defenses perform as well after taking one hit as they do having taken no hits—as well after two hits as after one, all the way up to the number of hits required for "mission kill." Similarly, the equations do not represent any interference (1) between carrier battle-groups as the number operating "in concert" grows, or (2) among power projection and fleet air defense operations on any carrier's busy deck. Perfect weather is, by exclusion, assumed, though foul weather would

---

firing from within the outer two, until hits per sortie are less than .5. Attacking Soviet platforms are assumed to be distributed evenly over whatever number of U.S. carriers are sent. The same barrier performance and overall hit probabilities for Soviet munitions are assumed for the Pacific offensive, but Soviet forces there number 104 bombers, 26 cruise missile submarines, and 62 torpedo submarines. Once fired, Soviet munitions must, in sequence (1) prove reliable, (2) penetrate the carrier's point defenses, (3) overcome electronic countermeasures and deception, and (4) hit the target. The overall hit probabilities given in table 18 are the products of these probabilities. They are assumed to be the same for Murmansk and Petropavlovsk and are as follows: for bombers, .9, .75, .5, .3; for cruise missile submarines .9, .75, .8, .1; for torpedo submarines .85, 1.0, .7, and .05.

When these values are applied in the calculation described above, 9 carriers for the Kola and 6 for the Pacific result (hits per carrier are six in each case). The force numbers for bombers are taken from John M. Collins, *U.S.-Soviet Military Balance 1980–1985* (Washington, D.C.: Pergamon-Brassey's, 1985), p. 147; a readiness level of 80 percent is assumed. Force numbers for cruise missile and torpedo submarines are from International Institute for Strategic Studies, *The Military Balance 1985–1986* (London: IISS, 1985), pp. 26–29. Sources for munitions per sortie are as follows. For bombers, International Institute for Strategic Studies, *The Military Balance 1986–1987* (London: IISS, 1986), p. 206; for cruise missile submarines: The Royal Ministry of Defence (Norway), Press and Information Office, "Development of the Soviet Forces in Our Sphere of Interest During the Past 20 Years," Current Defence Issues No. 0185 (April 1985), annex 6; and for torpedo submarines, *Jane's Fighting Ships 1986–87* (London: Jane's Publishing, 1986), pp. 544–55.

48   *Joshua M. Epstein*

Table 18. Summary of Assumptions for Kola Offensive

Soviet weapon type	Munitions launched per sortie	Initial attack force	Attrition rate per sortie (percent)	Overall hit probability per munition
Antiship missile bombers	2	200	57	.10
Cruise missile submarines	8	35	73	.05
Torpedo submarines	6	71	73	.03

Source: See note 62 in the text.

probably hurt carrier operations more than it would hurt Soviet land-based bomber operations—if for no other reason than that a land airfield does not pitch in rough seas.[63] Various threats to the U.S. carriers are also left out of account: Soviet surface cruisers, destroyers, frigates, mines, and tactical air forces. All these favorable assumptions obtain regardless of what numbers are applied in the calculation.

MODEL ASSUMPTIONS NUMERICALLY FAVORABLE TO THE NAVY. Beyond the favorable assumptions implicit in the computational procedure per se are numerical assumptions. These, again, seem favorable to the U.S. Navy. Boiled down, they appear in table 18.

First, future U.S. carrier fleets (for example, the 15-carrier fleet) are sent to do battle with current Soviet bomber and submarine forces. Obviously, if—as would have been more realistic—carrier requirements were assessed against future Soviet bomber and submarine forces, the number of carriers required would be greater.

Second, Soviet attrition rates are vastly higher than any recorded in recent military history, from the Battle of the Atlantic (for subs) to the Marianas Turkey Shoot (for air); in particular, U.S. anti-air performance is stellar. Here one is speaking of Soviet bomber attrition rates of 57 percent per sortie, far higher than the highest rates (36 percent) suffered by the United States in World War II, at the battle of Midway, June 4, 1942.[64] Soviet hit probabilities, by contrast, are positively lackluster. For air-delivered munitions they are .1, which is less than one-quarter of what U.S. precision-guided munitions achieved against bridges in Vietnam.[65]

63. It could, however, be argued that a carrier would be harder to find—and hence attack—in bad weather.
64. Jeffrey H. Grotte, *Alternative Surface Navy Force Structures for the Future*, IDA Paper P-1705 (Alexandria, Va.: Institute for Defense Analyses, 1983), p. 31.
65. See Epstein, *Measuring Military Power*, pp. 148–49.

All in all, then, it is difficult to believe that—while hardly realistic—the analysis is biased against the United States Navy. That, however, is what one must show to discredit the conclusions.

Even on these assumptions, for any confidence (carrier survival probabilities exceeding 20 percent) of success against the forces of the Kola complex and supporting air bases, the required number of carriers is 9. When the same analysis is done to determine the number required for equal confidence of survival against the Soviet Pacific Fleet, the result is 6.[66]

Adding the Navy's wartime requirements for 2 carriers apiece in the Indian Ocean, Mediterranean, and Eastern Pacific, and assuming generously that the Navy could keep 100 percent of its fleet on station in wartime,[67] *the maritime strategy carrier fleet totals 21, at incremental ten-year costs of about $158 billion.* If, perhaps more realistically, one assumes that only 75 percent of the fleet can be kept on station in war, the peacetime inventory needed to keep 21 carriers fighting is 28; 13 more than the 15-carrier fleet, and over $340 billion more in ten-year costs (table 19). Clearly, either fleet is out of the question budgetarily. For the Navy, the mismatch between strategy and forces could not be starker.[68] For the nation, however, this is not especially troublesome, since defensive carrier employment would be every bit as effective as offensive operations in accomplishing what is essential: protection of the sea-lanes.

Detailed analyses recently declassified demonstrate that the substitution of land-based for carrier-based aircraft would prove equally effective in addressing the bomber threat to convoys at one-fifth the cost.[69] In fact, on the basis of these assessments, the United States could efficiently secure the sea-lanes from attack with a fleet of as few as 8 carriers if land-based and other alternatives to carrier-based airpower

66. See note 62.

67. For the Navy's assumption that 100 percent of the fleet can be kept on station in war, see "Prepared Statement of Hon. John F. Lehman, Jr., Secretary of the Navy," in *Department of Defense Appropriations for 1987,* Hearings of the Subcommittee on the Department of Defense of the House Committee on Appropriations, 99 Cong. 2 sess. (GPO, 1986), p. 289.

68. The Navy's repeated claim that the maritime strategy is a strategy "for today," moreover, could not be further from the mark in this light.

69. Jerome Bracken and others, *Land-Based and Sea-Based Barrier Air Defense of the North Atlantic Sea Line of Communications,* IDA Report R-230 (Alexandria, Va.: Institute for Defense Analyses, 1977). Formerly secret; declassified December 31, 1985.

Table 19. U.S. Carrier Forces Required for Offensive and Defensive Sea Control

Item	Offensive (carrier intensive)		Defensive (land-based air intensive)	
Atlantic Sea Control	9		0	
Pacific Sea Control	6		2	
Indian Ocean and Arabian Sea	2		2	
Mediterranean	2		2	
East Pacific	2		2	
Total on station for global war	21		8	
Wartime on-station rate (percent)	100	75	100	75
Required peacetime inventory	21	28	8	11
Number beyond 15	6	13	−7	−4
Additional ten-year cost (billions of fiscal 1988 dollars)[a]	158	342	−53[b]	−30[b]

Source: See note 62.

a. Jerome Bracken and others, *Land-Based and Sea-Based Barrier Air Defense of the North Atlantic Sea Line of Communications,* IDA Report R-230 (Alexandria, Va.: Institute for Defense Analyses, 1977), p. D-20. When Department of Defense TOA (total obligational authority) deflators (grand total of 52.86) are used to convert fiscal 1977 to fiscal 1988 dollars, IDA's costs per battle group are $18.8 billion a year in investment and $0.75 billion a year in operation and support. TOA deflators are from OASD, *National Defense Budget Estimates for FY 1988/ 1989,* p. 52.

b. Operation and support only.

were fully exploited (table 19). Over ten years such approaches would cost more than $50 billion less than the 15-carrier fleet. A force of 12 carriers represents a compromise. In no event should Congress appropriate monies for further carrier construction.

Moreover, although the Navy has never convincingly argued that offensive operations against the Kola Peninsula would be more effective than defensive operations in protecting sea-lanes, even if one grants the necessity for such attacks, it still does not follow that carriers are a good buy. On a life-cycle cost basis, in fact, the aircraft carrier is overwhelmingly dominated by conventional cruise missile carrying aircraft and submarines (figure 6).[70]

70. This, in fact, addresses the Navy's argument that it would only send carriers against the Kola Peninsula—home of the Soviet Northern Fleet—after Soviet naval aviation had suffered severe attrition. With what weapons is this severe attrition accomplished? Why not apply more of those weapons (for example, conventional cruise missiles) and finish the job, rather than invest tens of billions to be able to finish it with carriers? (Of course, any set of assumptions that makes carrier offensives against the Kola Peninsula appear feasible will make carrier operations near the GIUK look easy by comparison.)

Figure 6. Cruise Missile Delivery Potential of Forces with Equal Life-Cycle Costs

Thousands of cruise missiles (or equivalents) delivered

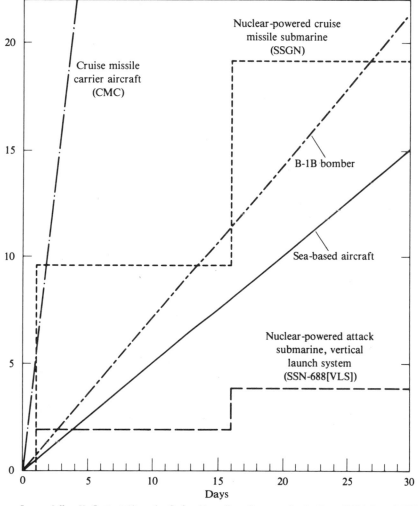

Source: Jeffrey H. Grotte, "Alternative Surface Navy Force Structures for the Future," IDA Paper P-1705 (Alexandria, Va.: Institute for Defense Analyses, Program Analysis Division, December 1983), p. 27.

SUBMARINE OFFENSIVES. Associated with the maritime strategy's offensive surface naval actions are offensive submarine operations that would aim to put Soviet nuclear ballistic missile submarines (SSBNs) at risk. There is every reason to believe this conventional counterforce campaign would be undertaken intentionally, as a deliberate attempt to degrade the Soviets' strategic retaliatory capability by conventional means.[71]

The U.S. Navy's wish to improve its capability to execute these operations underlies the administration's two-year request of $2.1 billion for the SSN-21 "Seawolf" nuclear-propelled attack submarine, the first of which would be procured in fiscal 1989.

First, trends in Soviet submarine quieting call into question the long-term feasibility of these counter-SSBN operations.[72] Second, even if they are feasible, are they advisable?

Assuming feasibility for the moment, such operations could prove escalatory: "a deliberate conventional campaign against Soviet SSBNs could be understood by the Soviets as the beginning of a damage-limiting strategic first-strike. . . even the appearance of such a campaign could trigger dire consequences."[73] The mere fact that U.S. nuclear weapons had not been used to destroy Soviet strategic weapons would not make the latter's annihilation any less momentous; Soviet assured destruction capabilities would be degraded. Under such circumstances, the prospect of Soviet escalation might well be raised. If so, American aircraft carriers operating in the vicinity of the Soviet homeland would themselves make attractive targets for Soviet nuclear response.[74]

The Navy argues that the aim of these subsurface offensives would be to force the Soviets into a defensive posture from which they could not threaten NATO's sea lines of communication. By the time the SSN-21 would be deployed in numbers, however, the Soviets might not feel under great pressure to cooperate by withholding their nuclear-powered attack submarines to defend their SSBNs. The passage north of Soviet SSBNs to the relatively safe shallow waters at the edge of the ice cap could be protected by other, smaller, submarines and airpower. And through quieting, these SSBNs will have been made inherently more

71. Admiral James D. Watkins, U.S. Navy,"The Maritime Strategy," *The Maritime Strategy* (Annapolis: U.S. Naval Institute, 1986), pp. 2–17, esp. pp. 11, 14, 17.

72. On attacking Soviet SSBNs, see Tom Stefanick, *Strategic Antisubmarine Warfare and Naval Strategy* (Lexington Books, 1987), chap. 6.

73. Barry R. Posen, "Inadvertent Nuclear War? Escalation and NATO's Northern Flank," *International Security*, vol. 7 (Fall 1982), p. 43.

74. As Bernard Brodie put it, "what better targets are there for such [tactical nuclear] weapons than our nice, big aircraft carriers." Letter from Bernard Brodie to Adm. Stansfield Turner, January 16, 1976, as quoted in Desmond Ball, "Nuclear War at Sea," *International Security*, vol. 10 (Winter 1985–86), p. 8.

The 1988 Defense Budget

difficult to attack.[75] The net result might be that the United States would squander the conventional sea control capabilities of its SSN force in a fruitless effort to attack Soviet SSBNs, while freeing the Soviets' best attack submarines to harass NATO's sea-lanes—exactly the reverse of the strategy's intent.[76]

Parallel arguments are offered to support offensive U.S. aircraft carrier operations against Soviet forces in the north. But if the cost of tying down Soviet air forces in the north with U.S. battle groups is four or five times the price of defeating those forces by using land-based tactical aircraft in NATO's center region, then the approach again is inefficient. More to the point, though, can the Navy be sure the Soviets would be tied down at all? Perhaps it is the United States and not the Soviet Union that has been lured into allocating vast sums to long-war, horizontal-counteroffensive naval capabilities when the main Soviet objective would be a short land war focused on Germany.

Sometimes the reinforcement of Norway (which fields a tough defense of its own) is offered as a justification for the maritime strategy. But it is not necessary to threaten the strategic nuclear retaliatory capabilities of the Soviet Union (that is, Soviet nuclear ballistic missile submarines) to reinforce Norway. Nor is it necessary to land Marines on the Kola Peninsula and outflank a Soviet overland threat to Norway. The terrain facing a Soviet land attack is formidable. The transportation system is sparse and vulnerable (bridges can be prechambered to accept explosives in crisis) and offers great leverage to a skillful defender, as the Finns proved to the Russians in the winter war of 1939–40. The Soviet amphibious threat to Norway, in turn, can be addressed by the Norwegian navy, defensive mining, and shore-based airpower and artillery, while the Soviet air threat can be met with land-based aircraft from upgraded Norwegian fields (with a U.S. reinforcement from Scotland or the south Norwegian Sea if necessary).

Finally, third world peacetime contingencies and "showing the flag"—

75. See Stefanick, *Strategic Antisubmarine Warfare*, chap. 6. The Soviets will also have deployed mobile land-based ICBMs, which substitute to some extent for SSBNs, and might permit a slightly more relaxed attitude about moderate SSBN attrition.

76. Moreover, even if the Navy could show that this approach was feasible and without nuclear risk, it would remain to be demonstrated that an offensive approach was less expensive than a defense of the sea-lanes farther south, using land-based antisubmarine forces, mining, and cheaper, diesel-powered, submarines operating near the GIUK gaps.

Table 20. Proposed Alterations to the Administration's Conventional Defense Plan, Fiscal Years 1988–89
Billions of dollars

Program	Action	Budget authority (050) savings 1988	1989
Navy			
2 nuclear aircraft carriers (CVNs)	Deny funding	0.7	0.8
Carrier service life extension program (SLEP)	Cancel	0.8	0.1
F-14, A-6 aircraft	Cut for 12 aircraft carrier battle groups	2.4	2.7
DDG-51 (Arleigh Burke) destroyer	Reduce by 2 a year	1.5	1.5
CG-47 (Aegis) cruiser	Reduce by 1 a year	1.0	0.9
SSN-21 nuclear attack submarine	Cancel procurement funds	0.3	1.5
SSN-688 nuclear attack submarine	Reduce to 2 a year	0.6	0.0
TAO fleet oiler	Reduce by 1 a year	0.1	0.1
V-22 aircraft	Cancel	0.5	0.7
Army and Air Force			
Advanced tactical fighter (ATF)	Freeze at 1987 level	0.3	0.5
LHX helicopter	Cancel and reprogram half to fixed-wing competition	0.2	0.3
AMRAAM (advanced medium-range air-to-air missile)	Freeze at 1987 level	0.2	0.3
Patriot air defense missile	Reduce to 500 a year	0.3	0.4
M2 Bradley fighting vehicle	Cancel; replace with improved TOW vehicle (ITV) and upgraded M113[a]	0.6	0.3
F-15 aircraft	Reduce growth to 28 a year	0.6	0.6
F-19 aircraft	Cancel	0.1	0.1
Follow-on forces attack/deep attack programs	Delay[b]	0.2	0.3
Low-technology defensive preparations	Instant antitank ditching, terrain modification, prechambering of bridges	−0.2	−0.2
Airbase survivability	Expand current program	−0.2	−0.2
Strategic mobility			
C-17 aircraft	Cancel	1.9	2.1
Fast sealift	Expand at 4 a year	−0.4	−0.4
Operation and maintenance	Alter funding[c]	2.4	2.5
Total savings in budget authority	. . .	13.9	14.9
Resulting savings in outlays	. . .	(4.8)	(9.4)

Sources: Department of Defense, *Program Acquisition Costs by Weapon System, Fiscal Years 1988 and 1989,* pp. 32, 33, 42, 48, 74, 81, 88, 89, 90, 95, 96, 99, 103, 142, 145, and *Fiscal Year 1984,* p. 103; and Federation of American Scientists.
    a. This option is discussed in Congressional Budget Office, *Reducing the Deficit: Spending and Revenue Options,* 1986 Annual Report, pt. 2 (CBO, 1986), pp. 50–51.
    b. See CBO, *Reducing the Deficit: Spending and Revenue Options,* 1987 Annual Report, pt. 2 (CBO, 1987), pp. 40–41. For a fuller elaboration of the follow-on forces attack strategy and the main criticisms that can be lodged against it, see Epstein, *The 1987 Defense Budget,* pp. 39–41.
    c. See CBO, *Reducing the Deficit: Spending and Revenue Options,* 1987 Annual Report, pt. 2, pp. 52–53.

peacetime presence—are given as rationales for the maritime strategy. But under the current budgetary constraints, the burden of proof is on the Navy to articulate (1) the number of simultaneous peacetime presence missions for which the United States should plan, (2) why a fleet of 12 carrier battle groups (and 4 surface action groups) should be inadequate to the task, and (3) why all the carriers must be 90,000-ton, rather than smaller, vessels.

CONCLUSIONS. The dominant issue, however, is the maritime strategy's contribution to conventional defense in the big contingencies, notably the conventional defense of Western Europe. And in that connection the basic point is that if NATO loses the short war (which the Soviets plan for), then long-war capabilities—of which navies are the exemplar—will be pointless. In effect, the maritime strategy represents a massive diversion of resources from the immediate defense of Western Europe into offensive surface and subsurface naval actions that are inefficient in accomplishing essential naval tasks (for example, the defense of sea-lanes) and that could prove escalatory on the generous assumption that they are feasible. Under current budgetary constraints, it is high time to abandon this risky and expensive approach. The administration's $1.4 billion two-year request to begin funding for 2 new large-deck nuclear-powered attack aircraft carriers should be denied, and other naval growth rates reduced to levels consistent with a 12-carrier-battle-group force structure. Procurement funding for the new SSN-21 submarine can be deferred, also without detriment to the Navy's ability to execute its essential missions in war or to support American foreign policy objectives in peace.

The complete set of conventional adjustments recommended in this section is shown in table 20.

Summation

The adoption of the nuclear and conventional proposals elaborated in this study would impose net reductions of $22.2 billion and $25.1 billion in defense budget authority in fiscal 1988 and 1989. Resulting levels of budget authority would be $289.8 billion ($100 million above a nominal freeze) and $307.3 billion. Growth rates, after inflation, would be − 4.3 percent and + 2.5 percent (table 21).

The composition of these reductions reflects priorities that differ sharply from those of the administration. First, to recall the budget

**Table 21. Recommended Adjustments to the Administration's Defense Program,
Fiscal Years 1988–89[a]**
Billions of dollars unless otherwise specified

Item	1988	1989
Savings in strategic nuclear programs	8.3	10.2
Savings in conventional programs	13.9	14.9
Total savings in budget authority	22.2	25.1
Resulting levels of budget authority	289.8	307.3
Percent real budget authority growth (year-to-year)	− 4.3	2.5
Total savings in outlays	7.0	14.8
Resulting levels of outlays	290.6	297.4
Percent real outlay growth (year-to-year)	− 1.6	− 1.3

Sources: Tables 3, 15, 20.
a. Adjustments to the National Defense Function (050).

categories discussed at the outset, the proposed reductions are focused
on the investment accounts, notably procurement and R&D. While
(because of relatively low outlay *rates*) they have only a limited immediate effect on the deficit, these reductions (because of their substantial
size) generate large outlay savings in the future. Deficit reduction would
gather momentum (a negative "bow wave," if you will) without detriment to the immediate combat capability of U.S. forces.

Although, by most accounts, strategic forces represent less than 20
percent of the defense budget, they absorb 60 percent of the reductions
proposed here for fiscal 1988. Conventional forces, in that sense, take
priority over strategic.

Within the strategic forces, full funding for the Trident submarine and
D-5 missile programs, for stealth and nonstealth cruise missiles, for the
B-1 bomber, and for completed deployment of 50 MX missiles will
provide robust prompt and delayed retaliatory capabilities against even
the hardest of Soviet targets. Further counterforce capabilities, in the
form of mobile Midgetman or rail-mobile MX, are unnecessary from the
standpoint of target coverage (the more so given the projected shrinkage
in the Soviet hard-target base), even on the questionable assumption of
survivability. Profound skepticism regarding the technical feasibility,
affordability, and stability of a transition to the world of "assured
survival" is evident in the sharp reductions proposed for the president's
strategic defense initiative. These measures—also out of concern for
strategic stability—would effectively preclude the early deployment of
space-based partial defenses. A prudent level of continuing research on

strategic defense would be sustained. The stealth *technologies* are funded (for instance, through the advanced cruise missile program), while the procurement of duplicative *platforms,* such as the stealth (advanced technology) bomber, is not.

Finally, within the nonnuclear sphere, the administration's request for tanks and antiarmor munitions is honored, and a cost-effective replacement for the Bradley fighting vehicle is provided. An additional heavy division equivalent would be created for NATO (from superfluous light divisions oriented toward the Persian Gulf), where defensive preparations, sealift, and fixed-wing close air support receive additional impetus. Improvements in NATO's (underrated) conventional defense capabilities would be more than paid for through reductions in inefficient strategic, tactical air, and, especially, naval programs.

512 927